O Cruel death
To please thy hungry pallet
Has crop't my lettice —
To make thy self a sallet

Faithful
UNTO
DEATH

OUR BELOVED PETS
MR. & MRS. A. G. WHITE

THE LOYALTY OF A DOG MAY WELL PUT
MOST MEN TO SHAME, FOR FEW ARE AS
LOYAL TO THEIR HEAVENLY MASTER AS
IS THE HUMBLE DOG TO HIS EARTHLY ONE

Faithful
UNTO
DEATH

**PET CEMETERIES,
ANIMAL GRAVES &
ETERNAL DEVOTION**

Paul Koudounaris

Contents

Introduction

In the Gatekeeper's Garden

Cherry was a good dog. A playful Maltese who wanted to be involved in anything and everything his family did, he was always the first to run downstairs to fetch the mail when it arrived at their home at 10 Cambridge Square in London. Scurrying back up the steps, he would deliver the letters to his mum, Emily Lewis-Barned, his tail wagging wildly as he anticipated his reward, the smile on her face as she reached down to pet him. And if her door was closed, he would push them under and then wait for her to come out. When visitors stopped by, he delighted in being the center of attention, playing soldier in a miniature army coat and helmet. But his greatest joy was the children, Amelia and Harry. He treasured the walks they would take to Hyde Park, where they could play together in the soft grass on warm summer days.[1]

Having lived a long and happy life, Cherry succumbed to old age in 1881. Tragic as the loss was for the Lewis-Barneds, there is, in and of itself, nothing remarkable in Cherry's story. His canine virtues notwithstanding, there have always been plenty of dogs like him—those that live for love, and whose passing rends the heart and leaves in its wake a trail of tears. Cherry would not ordinarily be remembered almost a century and a half later. His place in history was secured not through being a good dog, but rather as a consequence of a decision made upon his death.

The trips to Hyde Park were frequent enough that the family had become friendly with the gatekeeper, Mr. Winbridge, who lived in a cottage behind Victoria Gate. To outsiders he seemed an intimidating figure, tall in stature, with a thick gray beard, and a uniform of red waistcoat and

Image of Mr. Winbridge that appeared in a French article on his dog cemetery, published in 1899.

An early photo of the Hyde Park cemetery shows Cherry's grave in the front row, far right.

tall hat trimmed in gold. But to those who knew him, he was a most amiable fellow, a man who always offered a good word and kept a ready supply of lollipops on hand for the local children. At a loss for a way to memorialize Cherry, the Lewis-Barneds approached Mr. Winbridge with a request. Could they lay him to rest in the garden of the gatekeeper's cottage, just a stone's throw from the lawn that had been the little dog's favorite playground?

Mr. Winbridge agreed. A grave was dug, a funeral held, and a small headstone set in place, inscribed with the words, "Poor Cherry. Died 28 April 1881." No one could have guessed that Cherry's burial, a gesture of love on the part of his family and one of charity on the part of the gatekeeper, would turn out to be a revolutionary act. But as word spread that Cherry had been given a grave in the gatekeeper's yard, it wasn't long before other grieving pet owners began begging the same favor. Mr. Winbridge was of too great a heart to say no, and slowly his little plot was transformed into something that not only London, but also the entire Western world, had been unaware that it desperately needed. His garden became the first urban cemetery for pets.

There was, of course, nothing revolutionary about burying an animal. Entire animal necropoli had existed in the ancient world. Bubastis in Egypt comes to mind, the city of cats, where the ground was filled with feline mummies. There had been individual burials of famous animals too, such as Alexander the Great's favorite hunting dog, Peritas, given a grave at the gates of a town in India named in his honor. Some ancient gravestones still survive, such as a Roman plaque dated to the 2nd century CE, showing a dog of indeterminate breed standing

under a temple pediment, and bearing the inscription, "Helena, foster daughter, incomparable praiseworthy soul."[2]

Various animal burials were also recorded in Christian Europe. Among the extant grave markers is a sandstone tablet dated 1630 at the ruins of Winterstein Castle in central Germany, dedicated to a dog named Stuczel who was so clever that he was often sent the seven miles to Gotha to deliver letters from his master, a Thuringian Jägermeister, to Duke Ernest I.[3] And an impressive monument honoring Fortunatis, the 18th century's most remarkable pug, survives in Winnenden, Germany. The dainty dog accompanied Duke Karl Alexander during a siege of Belgrade in 1717; scared off by the din of battle, however, he turned tail and ran for home. This is hardly a surprising reaction, but succeeding was an extraordinary accomplishment since home was more than seven hundred miles away. Fortunatis's feat ensured his fame, and upon his death in 1733 a memorial stone over seven feet high was erected.[4]

We would err greatly, however, if we were to consider the necropolis at Bubastis as equal to a modern pet cemetery, or the grave markers for Helena, Stuczel, and Fortunatis to be evidence that ancient Rome or Baroque Germany had practices of pet ownership similar to ours. The vast majority of the animals found in Egyptian necropoli were raised by temples specifically to be sacrificed, and as for the individual grave markers, they are exceptional specifically because they are so rare. This is not to imply that the ancients were incapable of loving their animals as much as we are. Indeed, there is proof that many did. But our pets are of a different breed than their animal ancestors. They are a culturally specific phenomenon that pervades all levels of society, and we might argue that they do not truly qualify as animals at all, at least not in the minds of the people with whom they live. They exist in a kind of liminal space, remaining in body a member of the species to which they were born, but taking on a role that is nearly human in the lives of those who love them.

Stuczel's epitaph explains that he was offered a grave to prevent ravens from eating his cherished body.

The inscription on the stone dedicated to Fortunatis pledges that his memory will remain in this spot.

Pets as we know them are an invention of the 19th century, a product of the great social shift that saw people flock to big cities in the wake of the Industrial Revolution. Paris, for example, added nearly two and a quarter million people, while Greater London swelled by more than five million. New York City, meanwhile, grew from sixty thousand residents to three and a half million, an astounding increase of almost sixtyfold. Rural traditions of animal husbandry had no place in congested cities, but that didn't mean the new arrivals ceased to keep animals. There was an evolution in their relationship, however, as the cramped quarters of the modern metropolis drew people and animals closer than they had ever been, and not just physically, but emotionally.

Not only were people bonding with animals in an entirely new way, the vast panoply of cruelty to which they had been subjected for millennia was more on display than ever before—and becoming increasingly intolerable to wide swathes of the public. The 19th century gave birth to welfare organizations, starting in England in 1824 with the first Society for the Prevention of Cruelty to Animals. Such groups attempted to stop the heinous abuses suffered by animals as a source of cheap labor, and the victims were more than just stereotypical beasts of burden: even dogs and cats might be worked to death. The new movement stressed that they are sentient beings, and that cruelty towards them was a sign of degraded moral sensibility.

Showing kindness to animals, on the other hand, was promoted as a virtue, and one that brought great rewards. If we could understand their emotions, it was conjectured, it might help us establish meaningful attachments that could in turn make our own lives richer. This all seems self-evident now, but these were entirely new ideas at the time.

Pitched battles were fought, with those who stood as champions of animals forced to persevere despite mockery being heaped upon them. Yet their efforts resulted in milestones that resonate to the present day. In the United States, Charles Burden brought a suit against a neighbor in Johnson County, Missouri, who had shot his favorite dog, Drum, in 1869.[5] Taking such a matter to court was odd enough, but Burden was suing not just for the replacement value of his hound. In addition, he wanted damages for what he had lost: the love and affection of an animal companion. The matter seemed laughable until George Vest, a Missouri senator and himself a dog lover, addressed the jury with one of the great orations in American legal history.

"The best friend a man has in this world may turn against him and become his enemy," he began, stressing the inconstancy of man. "Those who are nearest and dearest to us, those . . . who are prone to fall on their knees to do us honor when success is with us may be the first to throw the stone of malice when failure settles its cloud upon our heads." In comparison, however, "The one absolutely unselfish friend that a man can have . . . the one that never proves ungrateful or treacherous, is his dog."

"A man's dog stands by him in prosperity and in poverty, in health and in sickness," Vest continued. "He will sleep on the cold ground, where the wintry winds blow and the snow drives fiercely, if only he may be near his master's side. He will kiss the hand that has no food to offer, he will lick the wounds and sores that come in encounters with the roughness of the world." Vest finished his summation by appealing to emotion, arguing that in the end, it is a dog's loyalty only that can be counted eternal. "When all other friends desert, he remains . . . and when the last scene of all comes, and death takes the master in its embrace and his body is laid away in the cold ground . . . there by his graveside will the noble dog be found, his head between his paws, his eyes sad but open in alert watchfulness, faithful and true even to death."

Vest drew tears from those assembled, and won Burden's case. He also gave

birth to a popular new phrase: "A dog is man's best friend." It was a precedent-setting victory, the first time in history a court of law had affirmed that an animal's worth is more than just material. On another front, the nascent welfare movement took on the vivisectionists who used animals, strapped to tables in writhing pain, for anatomical demonstrations, and in the process erected the first great monument to honor animals' rights. A seven-foot-high granite fountain topped by a bronze terrier was placed in a clearing in Battersea Park in London as a posthumous memorial to an anonymous brown dog that fell victim to a scalpel at University College London. On its base ran an inscription pleading that humanity not be reserved for humans alone: "Men and Women of England, how long shall these things be?"

Inventing the modern pet involved more than just acknowledging the value of animals as companions, however, or insisting that they receive humane treatment. We cannot, for instance, overlook the fact that pets have evolved into a huge industry, one that generates around a hundred billion dollars a year in the United States alone. This was also a creation of the 19th century. For the first time, manuals were published on the feeding and care of domestic animals. Their grooming became an issue of often obsessive importance, with various supplies suddenly available for home use, and the upscale market served by the introduction of salons. And animal couture, which previously would have been an oxymoron to anyone save perhaps royalty, became big business, with quarterly 'look books' offered by Parisian design houses.

Pet ownership grew at such a rapid pace that by the early 20th century critics lamented what it might portend. "The dog is fast supplanting, in the aristocratic homes of Europe and America, the honored presence of children," one noted with alarm.[6] The author's apprehension was unfounded. Humans didn't stop having children, although pets had become children too, of a different kind. How we bond with, live with, and care for domestic animals were all changing indelibly, and it is only within that context that we can understand the importance of Cherry's burial, and why it stands out from the countless interments of animals that had come before.

The invention of pets may have created a category of animal that was accepted as a beloved family member, yet their status came with one, shall we say, grave exception. Society was willing to accept only so much encroachment on what was considered human privilege, and a dignified burial was a line that even many sympathetic people were loath to see breached. Like Cinderella's coach, it was as if, when the clock struck the final hour, pets reverted to base matter—regardless of how they lived, the consensus was that they did not deserve to be commemorated in the same way as a human family member.

Even a century and a half later the stigma still lingers, leaving many people lost in quiet grief. In the 19th century the propriety of mourning a pet

A mid-20th-century photo shows visitors at a memorial placed where Drum's body was discovered.

The Brown Dog's monument was later targeted by vandals opposed to the animal rights movement.

was an entirely new and puzzling problem manifesting itself across society on a massive scale. And this is why, even though Cherry's funeral was accompanied by none of the hoopla that surrounded the trial of Drum or the battle over vivisection, it was nonetheless an equally important milestone. As Cherry was joined by Prince, Spot, Yum Yum, and a few hundred others, Mr. Winbridge's little plot was transformed not just into a cemetery, but into a statement. His garden became a visible message in a public park in the world's largest city, proclaiming that among the rights due an animal that had been loved as a family member are last rites, that pets deserve a death with dignity. That is why Cherry's burial was revolutionary, and why the cemetery in Hyde Park served as an inspiration for those that would follow, in Europe and the United States in the late 19th century, and then across the world during the 20th.

As the idea spread, it evolved to encompass any number of geographic variations and spiritual beliefs to honor any number of species. In some areas, local custom involves hand-painted tributes. Certain cemeteries are exclusive to specific breeds. Post-apocalyptic desert landscapes host sprawling off-the-grid burial grounds. There are temples dedicated to mourning rituals for pets, and others that maintain columbaria to store their cremated ashes. But no matter how different the places they are found and how varied their traditions— from Alaska to Australia, from the jungles of Bali to the Bolivian altiplano, from central Cairo to the Catalan coast, and on down through the atlas—they all strive for the same goal: affirming the respect and dignity due a pet upon its passing. And it all started in the gatekeeper's garden.

A Hyde Park maintenance worker tending the graves of the dog cemetery in the 1930s.

Cherry is still buried in Hyde Park, even though only the base of his gravestone remains (center).

SWEETY
طماطوطو
Thank You For Being You

November 1997
18 June 2018

BUGZY
2007-2021

SOSO
We All Love you
I Love you

Kasper

PET
SNAIL
JONNY
HE LIVED
LIFE WELL
2016

Lucas
Tu nunca morirás
en nuestros cora-
zones, eres
eterno por cada
parte que nos
diste en vida.

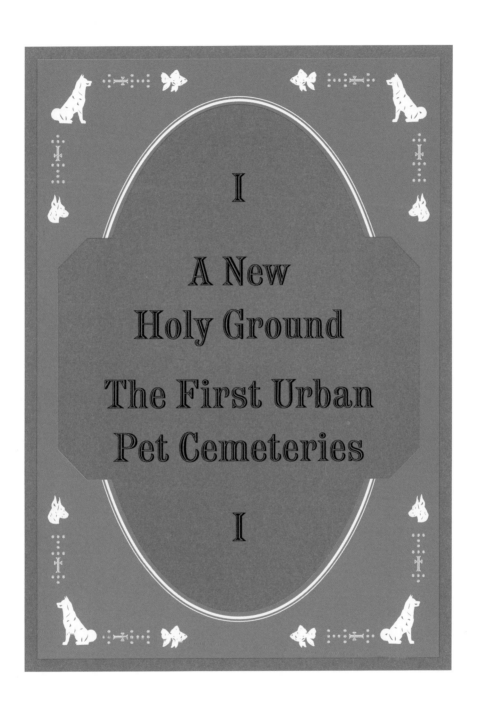

I

A New
Holy Ground

The First Urban
Pet Cemeteries

I

Bones of Contention:
Dead Pets in the 19th Century

The cemetery in the yard behind Mr. Winbridge's cottage was a quaint and tidy affair, the little graves separated into neat rows and cordoned off with rope-edge tiles to give each family a place to leave flowers. With its miniature headstones of simple and unostentatious shapes, there was a precious quality to it, almost like a cemetery for a dollhouse. Mr. Winbridge performed all the burials himself, and he never charged for the plot or his labor, the only cost to a pet's family being whatever grave marker they chose to provide. The term "pet cemetery" was not yet in use in the 19th century, so the public instead called the grounds the Hyde Park Dog Cemetery, although the proprietor himself lovingly referred to it as his "canine necropolis."[1]

It was not the first time that term had been used in London, however, and it had previously not been so loving. Enfield, a borough in the north of the city, was the "canine necropolis" in the days before Mr. Winbridge. It was there that dead pets could be disposed of for industrial purposes. Around 750 dogs a week were taken in for rending, with most of them broken down into manure. Their bodies were laid flat and chemicals applied, and then turned over "like toast when done on one side" and the process repeated, creating a putrid stench that permeated the area and brought consistent complaints from residents.[2] As grotesque as it sounds, there was nothing unique about Enfield. Every big city had such a district, where dogs and cats that had left tearful human companions behind were processed alongside dead livestock.

Never has the torment of an animal's passing been more painful than in the big cities of the 19th century, where it was exacerbated by a total lack of sympathetic options for disposal of the body. Offering a pet for rending was at least officially sanctioned, although it was so unthinkably callous that many people instead chose to toss their recently deceased pets into rivers. That seems preferable only in comparison, and it is hardly less heartbreaking to picture a grieving owner raising the still warm corpse of a beloved Rover into the air and hurling it forth to a watery grave. The body would hit with a splash and perhaps float for an excruciating moment before slowly starting to sink. Bubbles would surround the corpse as dirty water entered to weigh it down, followed by the last glance at what was perhaps the best friend a person knew, a head or rump disappearing beneath the surface. In Paris, an estimated five thousand dogs a year wound up in the Seine, the tragedy for their owners compounded by the civic cost, with the bodies polluting the river and resulting in 4,000 francs in annual cleanup fees.[3]

There was plenty of cemetery space, of course, the problem being that it was intended for humans. Cemeteries in the Western world had traditionally been considered *terra sancta*, holy ground, specifically for members of a church congregation, which left animals out. And even after the advent of large, modern, non-denominational cemeteries, the stigma against the burial of pets alongside humans was persistent enough that the common opinion was that their presence defiled the grounds. Of course, that didn't stop people from trying to inter them, but the result if caught was often a debacle, such as befell a Glasgow woman who wished to bury a cat named Tom in 1885.[4] Upon his passing, she had an undertaker prepare a small coffin, and then laid his body in state in her home. Word spread and a large number of visitors came by, the cat's wake being a novelty about which people were curious. Up to that point there is no record of any ill will, but that changed when the woman had the coffin moved to a plot she owned in a nearby cemetery.

Onlookers became agitated as the coffin entered the grounds. They did not want Tom buried there, and they were vocal in making the point. Fearing the situation might get out of control, the gravedigger closed the gate, but by then the crowd had become a mob and began to scale the wall. Denouncing the burial as a disgrace, someone grabbed the little coffin, broke it open, and pulled out the body of the cat. Police arrived to restore order, and Tom's corpse was recovered and returned to his mistress, who we must assume was in a terrible state owing to the rude behavior visited upon her beloved cat. The woman was escorted back to her home, and when the crowd refused to disperse a police constable was posted to guard against further violence.

There were other incidents that were nearly as bad, including one in Bucharest in 1899, when a crowd reported to be in the thousands blocked a man from taking his dog to a cemetery. In this case, when the police arrived it was

Women arranged in a triangular composition mourn a beloved dog in this hand-tinted, 19th-century photo.

 they who seized the body, taking it by force and unceremoniously throwing it onto a rubbish heap.[5] Simply put, animals have always been an unwanted presence in cemeteries intended for humans, and few have successfully been interred in them. Cremation would nowadays seem the obvious solution, but was not a viable option at the time. It was rare to cremate even the human dead until the latter part of the century, and most pet owners considered conferring a beloved animal to the fire no less cruel than rending—it provoked a collective "wail of horror," as a contemporary put it.[6]

Of course, not everyone felt that way. In London, "an enormously rich woman," as she was identified, not only had her Yorkshire terrier cremated, but also paid more than six hundred pounds for a cinerary urn in the shape of a miniature sedan chair. Inlaid with rubies, emeralds, and pearls, it contained a human skull in its interior, atop a crystal jar holding the dog's ashes.[7] But even people who might choose the flames would find that cremation was not always practical. At the time, there were no crematories dedicated to animals, so one for humans would have to be hired, which presented a further problem since the operators would not want word to get out that their ovens were also serving pets. Money was of course a great boon, and in the case of the Yorkshire terrier probably went a long way towards assuaging any concerns of the crematory operator, although we are thereby limiting cremation to a small, well-heeled group.

Taxidermy presented another option, and while stuffed Victorian-era lap dogs do survive, it was not a particularly appealing choice for domestic companions. It was first of all expensive, but even the vast majority of wealthy owners declined to have their pets stuffed. As a means of memorial, taxidermy suffered then from the same issue it suffers from now: many people find it distinctly creepy to have a dead animal "live on" in their home, its once-vivid eyes replaced by glass, perpetually staring blankly into space. In terms of both cost and concept, taxidermy was simply an uncomfortable option for most.

People living in the countryside, on the other hand, had a distinct advantage in finding palatable solutions. With ample space at their disposal, it became common, especially in England, for animal lovers who owned large estates to establish their own private cemeteries, a trend that began in the late 18th century and continued into the 20th. By far the most extensive early example was established by Frederica Charlotte, Duchess of York. Prussian by birth, she was inspired by the example of her grand-uncle, Frederick the Great, who had a small graveyard at Sans Souci—his rococo palace in Potsdam—where he buried eleven hounds. Frederica far outdid his efforts, however. Her love for the companionship of animals was said to be the result of her distaste for the company of her husband, and she was known to keep forty dogs at a time, along with cats and even a few monkeys. More than a hundred animals were given graves at her Oatlands Park estate in Weybridge, Surrey.

Sadly, time has not been kind to the duchess's cemetery. The burial grounds were built over, and the surviving gravestones have been rearranged and are badly weathered. But a well-preserved example of these early private cemeteries is found at Wrest Park in Silsoe, Bedfordshire, on the estate of the de Grey family, the ancestral Earls of Kent. The first interment that can be clearly dated is for Nissy in 1816, and he was eventually joined by fifteen companions, most buried by Annabel de Grey, the widow of Earl Frederick Cowper. These include a dog with the now awkward-sounding epitaph "In Memory of Little Dick," Annabel's "favourite," according to the inscription, even though Lancey, buried in 1875, and Douban, in 1876, were also eulogized as her "favourite"— either she was a capricious mistress or her dogs gained favor quickly.

The headstones at Wrest are ringed around a pedestal topped with a sculpture of a recumbent dog, a reminder that dogs were the animals of choice. Indeed, both in Britain and on the Continent they represent the vast majority of 19th-century burials. A smattering of graves for cats and birds can also be found on estates, however, along with a few surprising choices that we would regard as unlikely pets. At Rousham House in Oxfordshire, for example, a headstone dated 1882 is dedicated to a cow named Faustina Gwynne, who had gained the heart of her owner through her habit of chasing the neighbors. The most unlikely of all, however, is in the Gloucestershire village of Blockley, where a grave marked the last resting place of a trout. A stream ran through the property of William Keyte, who had developed an affection for the

Three children pantomime a funeral as a tribute to
a dead rabbit in a studio photo from around 1900.

fish, which he managed to tame. The grave itself was dug in the front garden of Keyte's cottage, but since the marker was made of wood, it was later relocated to the cottage's interior in order to preserve it. The inscription reads:

MEMORY OF THE OLD FISH
UNDER THE SOIL
THE OLD FISH DO LIE
20 YEARS HE LIVED
AND THEN DID DIE.
HE WAS SO TAME
YOU UNDERSTAND
HE WOULD COME AND
EAT OUT OF YOUR HAND.
DIED APRIL 20TH 1855
AGED 20 YEARS.

Some of the graves on English estates were ostentatious, such as the one honoring Lord Byron's Labrador retriever, Boatswain. Like his master, the dog had a wild streak. He would pick fights with whatever animals he could find and was seized by madness in 1808 after a scuffle with a rabid adversary. Byron stayed by his side until the end, after which he devised a monumental memorial in the main yard of Newstead Abbey, his ancestral home in Nottinghamshire. A rectangular stone block topped by a trophy, it carries on one face a lengthy inscription declaring Boatswain to have been possessed of "Beauty without Vanity, Strength without Insolence, Courage without Ferosity [sic], and all the virtues of Man without his Vices." It concludes with the epitaph, "To mark a friend's remains these stones arise; I never knew but one—and here he lies."

Most pet owners preferred to avoid such extravagance, however, and as the century progressed the trend was increasingly towards discretion. Mourning rites themselves could be elaborate, with deceased pets photographed on lace-covered pillows as though they were in blissful slumber, and many owners taking clippings of hair to place in gold lockets. But these trappings were kept

The sculpted dog at the Wrest Park cemetery was added to provide a point of central focus.

Little Dick was one of several favored dogs of Lady Annabel Cowper to be buried at Wrest.

discreet, and burials were set on remote sections of land at a remove from potential visitors. They often so mimicked the look of human cemeteries as to be mistaken for them. When Lady Palmerston visited Wrest, for instance, she spied the dogs' cemetery in the distance and commented, "How I do pity poor Anne, living alone at Wrest, surrounded by all those graves of her family," completely unaware of what she had actually seen.[8]

This desire for secrecy lay in an issue we have already noted: mourning a pet as one might a human was a step too far for much of the public. In an age of stiff upper lips, it could lead to accusations of over-sentimentality, and in the worst case might damage the owner's reputation. The Duchess of York's animal cemetery, for example, was widely lampooned. Lord Macaulay referred to it as "that most singular monument of human folly," and further quipped that, "even a sensible person might have a fondness for a dog, but the Duchess loved more dogs than anyone could reasonably love people."[9]

Meanwhile, in 1880 a woman in Birmingham was lambasted by the press after ordering a coffin and funeral cards for her dog. "It is superfluous to affirm that the owner of that lamented Fido is a maiden lady," read one barb, the implication being that what the poor woman truly wanted was a husband, but failing to find one had misdirected her affections towards a dog.[10] This kind of sexism—a belief that women were emotionally weaker and therefore more likely to mourn an animal—was typical of the time, even if it neglected historical reality. After all, such warlords as Alexander the Great and Frederick the Great had both loved their dogs enough to provide them with graves. Be that as it may, not only was the effect of such a prejudice insulting to women, it also discouraged men from openly grieving animals through fear of being mocked as effeminate.

Given the obstacles one had to navigate in order to handle a pet's passing with dignity, city dwellers needed to be creative. It was best to bury a pet in secret,

OVERLEAF: *The marker for William Keyte's trout, gravestones for the Duchess of York's menagerie at Oatlands Park, plus memorials at Dunham Massey, Exbury, Scarborough, Crinkle Park, and Knaresborough.*

Vår älskade katt

Zorro

18 år

usually under the cover of night and in a secluded spot, such as a remote section of a public park. We will never know how many graves might be hidden under Battersea Park in London or Parc Monceau in Paris, but we are at least offered a tantalizing hint by the Djurgården in Stockholm, the one such surreptitious burial place that eventually evolved into a legitimate pet cemetery. Formerly a royal hunting ground on the outskirts of Stockholm, by the 19th century the land had become a seldom-visited woodland park. It has been reputed that the first grave there was for a dog named Nero, interred in a clearing by a group of soldiers who had adopted him as a mascot after the death of his owner, the playwright August Blanche, in 1868.[11]

It is easy to see why the spot became popular among pet owners. No road ran nearby, and rows of tall trees protected the clearing from onlookers. In this case, the site continued in use as a burial ground long enough to be legislated as an official pet cemetery in the mid-20th century, and it is now openly filled with loving grave markers. The oldest date only to the 1950s, however, and the exact locations of those prior, be they in the hundreds or even thousands, remain a mystery. Those digging new graves periodically report discovering old bones, but, as products of an age when such things were best kept secret, none of them come from known interments.

But the cemetery behind Mr. Winbridge's cottage in Hyde Park offered the promise of a new type of *terra sancta*, one explicitly for animals, where their burials would no longer have to be hidden. Not only would cemeteries built on this model make it feasible for city dwellers to openly pay last respects to their pets, there was a strength in numbers as the little graves all grouped together struck a sympathetic chord with the public and were more praised than demeaned. The press affectionately referred to the new cemetery as the "Frogmore of poor bow-wow," in reference to the Frogmore Mausoleums and Burial Ground near Windsor Castle.[12] "There is nothing absurd in the erection of these little white stones," a reporter explained, "they are simple tokens of honest affection, and those who have loved their dogs will understand what a world of sorrow and regret they signify."[13]

Of course, the problem had never been with people who understood, but rather with those who didn't, and it was to them that reporters pointedly directed their commentary. "There is, indeed, little to differentiate in sentiment this burial-place from that in which loving hands consign the remains of loved human bodies," wrote one, stressing the dignity and solemnity of the grounds. He continued by emphasizing how there is "nothing obtrusive or objectionable about the modest canine Elysian Field of Hyde Park." It is a "graceful and

PREVIOUS: *A modern grave at Djurgården, among the oldest animal cemeteries still in use.*

By the late 19th century, the dog cemetery had filled Mr. Winbridge's yard in Hyde Park.

harmless custom to bury pet dogs," he added, concluding that, "as a tribute to the affectionate faithful and 'friend of man' no objection can be raised."[14]

The burial ground was conceded by all to be lovely. Meticulously tended by Mr. Winbridge, it was grown around by ivy and laurel, with berries from holly trees providing a dash of red among the sea of green, and the headstones piled thick with violets, tulips, and lilies. Typical of Victorian stoicism, the messages on the stones were often muted, as most owners offered little more than a name and perhaps a date. Others broke ranks to proclaim the honest grief of a pet's passing, however, and a visitor today can still feel their pain. "These little lives, so short in years as the flowers that bloom awhile, are gone and we are left in tears," one reads, while another is dedicated "To our gentle lovely little Blenheim, Jane—she brought the sunshine into our lives, but she took it away with her."

In addition to Cherry, the Lewis-Barneds laid to rest two more dogs, including a Yorkshire terrier named Zoe, so beloved that the family compiled her memoirs under the title *The True History of the Little Dog Zoe, and Her Holidays and Travels*. Buried in 1892, her headstone reads, "As deeply as ever dog was mourned, for friendship rare by her adorned." Other owners prayed for reunion, with such inscriptions as, "In memory of our darling little Bobbit. When our lonely lives are over and our spirits from this earth shall roam, we hope he'll be there waiting to give us a welcome home." Another, for Moussoo, prophesied that "there are men both good and wise who say that dumb creatures we have cherished here below shall give us kindly greeting when we pass the golden gate."[15]

CHAPTER I

"WITT"
BEST FRIEND I EVER HAD
DIED JUNE 1895.

E. GRAY

Despite being titularly a dog cemetery, canines didn't entirely rule the roost at Hyde Park, as a few cats were granted burials as well. These included a tabby named Chinchilla, who in 1895 was the subject of considerable controversy. The cat had been poisoned, although its cause of death was not the issue, the problem being rather its headstone, which bore words that "consigned to dreadful torture hereafter the dreadful assassin," as one person reported. Or as Mr. Windbridge described it, the inscription "cursed the murderer in his uprising and downsitting. It cursed him on earth and it cursed him in hell . . . it was the sort of curse that made you blind and took your breath away."[16]

Such a description certainly whets the appetite. Unfortunately for those who like curses, it was deemed inappropriate for a public space by the Duke of Cambridge, who served as Ranger of Hyde Park. He ordered it removed, and decency prevented the original words from being recorded. Its replacement bore a more staid inscription: "God restoreth thee to me, your ever loving mistress." The cat's owner wasn't quite done cursing, however, having inquired of a scholar from the British Museum about curses from ancient Chaldea. He suggested one that he assured her was potent, and it was added to the gravestone in cuneiform.[17]

This too caused consternation, but since no one save an archeologist could decipher its meaning the new stone was allowed to stay. The cat's owner was at least offered that much satisfaction.

PREVIOUS AND ABOVE: *The gravestones at Hyde Park have suffered from decades of neglect, although the graves themselves are still present, with a few hundred markers surviving.*

Unfortunately, the mysterious sigils were likewise never recorded, and are now entirely illegible. Was it a single-use curse, intended to fade after being cast? Or did the characters themselves simply fall victim to the curse of moss and lichen? Whatever the case, Hyde Park's most intriguing gravestone inscription has been lost to history.

 ## *Topper on the Bottom:* Social Status and the Spread of Pet Cemeteries

Mr. Winbridge continued to bury animals until his death on New Year's Day, 1899, at the age of eighty-six. By then, the available space in his garden was exhausted, with over three hundred graves and the animals stacked three deep in some of them. Even so, a few more burials were managed until 1903, when a request to gain additional space within the park was denied and the cemetery was finally declared closed. By this time, however, most new burials had been shifted to Molesworth, a village in Huntingdonshire, about an hour north of London by train. The first was recorded on June 6, 1903, for a terrier named Freddie, and within a decade the new cemetery had already far surpassed the old in number of burials.

Molesworth was also titled a dog cemetery, but the grounds were open from the start to the full gamut of animals, and this no doubt aided its rapid growth. Early cat fanciers were patrons, among them Mrs. Alice McLaren Morrison, whose collection of felines was the most impressive in Britain. She had traveled to India and brought back several exotic cats, eventually establishing a cattery that included blue ribbon–winning felines from Iran, Russia, and China. The cemetery also provided eternal peace to rabbits, parrots, snakes, monkeys, and mice.

While the burial grounds in Hyde Park had begun as an act of charity, Molesworth was conceived from the outset as a commercial venture. A price list detailed the various options, with graves ranging from 5 to 13 shillings depending on size. In addition, there was an annual maintenance fee of 1 pound 10 shillings if one wanted turf and bulbs, or a discounted rate for plain turf. Mr. Gray, the proprietor, would meet mourners at Kimbolton Station with a donkey cart, ready to carry the coffins containing their pets to the graveside, where they would be lowered into the ground with their heads pointed to the west, the direction of the setting sun. He personally led memorial services, wearing somber clothing and a velvet smoking cap.[18]

Like Hyde Park, Molesworth had its share of noteworthy inscriptions. Those remarked upon by visitors included, "If love could save you thou hadst not died," "Sleep my darling, sleep, your memory we shall always keep," and

IN
MEMORY OF DEAR
FITZ
WHO WAS A GOOD
SPORTSMAN & A MOST
FAITHFUL COMPANION
NEARLY 17 YEARS
& Mrs SHIRLEY

The Lodge
Victoria Gate
Hyde Park
W.2.
6/5/37

Dear Madam

Am enclosing
sketch of your Doggie's Memorial
as it will appear when finished
and put up, and which I hope
you will like.

I remain Madam
Yours truly
J.Gray.

"No need for a weapon with which to defend, if you only had him as your loyal friend." But unlike its predecessor, where small graves were the norm, Molesworth was a place where elites could flaunt their status and indulge their deceased pets with grand displays. The centerpiece of the grounds was a huge cross dedicated to all the animals interred there, commissioned by a wealthy woman whose identity was never revealed, and bearing a quote from Job 12:10: "In the Lord's hand is the soul of every living thing." Individual graves, meanwhile, were variously decorated with marble columns, arches, and fine sculptures. There was even a mausoleum with stained-glass windows for a dog named Tantalizing Tommy, who had died in Sorrento, Italy, and whose body had been shipped back to England.

This extravagance was no doubt part of the reason why Molesworth appealed to foreign luminaries looking for burial spots for their favored animals. These included no less than King Albert I of Belgium and princes Aphas and Chulas of Siam, who buried a dog named Tony there. Nicknamed To-To, his breed is not recorded; but the princes apparently owned him equally, and his gravestone explained that he was the "Sweetest and nicest doggie who was good as gold, bright as silver, sharp as steel. He is gone far too soon, our loss is irreparable, our profound grief inconsolable, his loss remains forever unfilled in our hearts."

Such aristocratic burials make the point that while the early English pet cemeteries were indeed a milestone in the evolution of domestic animals, they were not a democratic space. They were instead decidedly for the use of the

PREVIOUS: *One of the gravestones discovered when the current owners of Molesworth cleared the brush.*

This note from Mr. Grey accompanied his hand-drawn design for the grave of the dog pictured.

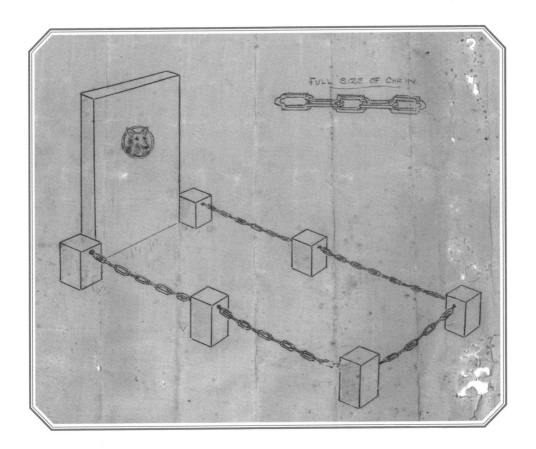

upper crust. This should not demean the genuine emotion involved—the love and grief were real—but, at the same time, being able to offer one's animal a grave in a cemetery also amounted to a final act of conspicuous consumption for pets that had spent a lifetime being pampered. Attendees at funerals were expected to wear mourning clothes, the bodies of dogs or cats were dressed in velvet robes or other costly garments, and carriages employed to transport the animals were bedecked with floral wreaths. One typical burial in Hyde Park was witnessed by an onlooker, who described a procession including a butler "of stately and grave demeanor," then nurses and ladies' maids following the dog's owner, and finally children walking two by two, everyone dressed in finery.[19]

The average Fido with a working stiff as an owner was not necessarily welcome in such cemeteries. Indeed, applications for interments behind Mr. Winbridge's cottage wound up far surpassing the available space, and the bulk of them had to be turned down. The extent to which these cemeteries were class conscious becomes painfully apparent in the curious case of a mixed-breed terrier named Topper, a police dog who had served as a mascot of the bobbies patrolling Hyde Park.

Topper was a genuine mutt, but he was nevertheless accepted for burial by Mr. Winbridge. Presumably this was done as a favor to the officers, who no doubt would have been on personal terms with the gatekeeper. Topper's burial soon

became something of a scandal in the canine world, however, as the poor dog was posthumously attacked in 1893 by a correspondent for *Strand Magazine*, who took exception to his place in the cemetery. The reporter accused the dog of having been "insufferably vulgar, with a bad strain in him which seems to have run through every line of his character."[20] He was prone to "deplorable self-indulgence" and "disgraceful habits," the author continued. To further Topper's disrepute, it was claimed he had "Bohemian tastes, and delighted in roaming about at night when all well-conducted dogs are in bed and asleep."[21]

In the single surviving photo of Topper, posed with the Hyde Park police unit he looks innocent enough, making the vitriol with which he was attacked even more perplexing. There is an almost surreal quality to such slander. "Bohemian tastes?" It hardly sounds possible that such complaints are even being made against a dog. The caricature drawn is of a picaro of the worst type, completed by accusing Topper himself of having been a snob. Yes, the reader was assured, this simple terrier was "a snob of the lowest and most contemptible kind," a confounding charge since it is quite clear that the snobbery was on the author's side, not Topper's.[22]

Deciphering the diatribe, the real problem was one of class. Pet-keeping in the 19th century very much reflected the social hierarchy, and a proper dog, like a proper gentleman, came with a pedigree, in order to best reflect the status and aspirations of its human counterpart. The obsession was so great that the majority of our known dog breeds date from the 19th century: in 1788, the Comte de Buffon, the great dog expert of his era, could name only fourteen, whereas by 1899 the veterinary pioneer Jean Pierre Mégnin was able to compile a list of two hundred. As the author of *Man's Friend, the Dog* queried in 1891, "no one would plant weeds in a flower garden . . . [so] why have mongrels as pets?"[23] Topper was very much a weed in Mr. Winbridge's garden.

But not only was Topper of muddled breeding, he had lived a life in which—Heaven forbid—he was free to simply act like a dog, rather than live restrained by the gilded manacles of Victorian pampering. "Proper" dogs in London frequented such salons as the Dogs' Toilet Club on New Bond Street, a veritable temple of canine cleanliness where they dined on sweetmeats while they waited for their turn to be washed with a warm-water spray and egg yolks, or have their claws clipped and polished. Topper, on the other hand, had to be content to lick himself clean. And whereas high-class dogs wore traveling coats ordered from the Continent, Topper's traveling coat was his bare fur. Like a coal miner at a cotillion, he was outclassed and out of place among the well bred canines from prominent families he was buried alongside.

*Initially mocked, Topper's grave stood the test of time
and is still present at Hyde Park.*

Indeed, what is known of the roster of interments in Hyde Park is impressive. There were highly valued show dogs that had taken home many hundreds of pounds in prizes. The head of the family that had buried Cherry and started it all, Israel Lewis-Barned, had an "esquire" after his name and was the son of a banking scion, although he hardly rated in comparison to some of those whose pets were nearby. Prince, for instance, killed by the wheel of a carriage on Bayswater Road and buried just a few graves over, had been owned by none other than Prince George, grandson of King George III, commander-in-chief of the British Army, and the park's own warden in his role as Duke of Cambridge.

This is nearly as high as it gets on the British social ladder, but the highest rungs may have been represented in the cemetery as well. It is notable that most of the headstones at Hyde Park do not list the names of owners. This was apparently to protect the privacy of high-ranking persons. Could some

A dog is lowered into a grave at an early 20th-century pet cemetery in Stahnsdorf, Germany.

of these dogs have belonged to the Crown? It was common knowledge that Queen Victoria had buried several of her own pets on the grounds of Windsor Castle, but it was also whispered that some of the more recently deceased had been interred in Hyde Park, as well as dogs owned by her daughter-in-law, the future Queen Alexandra.[24]

Sadly, there seems to have been a common opinion that mongrels like Topper did not warrant the honor of a burial. From an aristocratic point of view, dogs of his sort could be tossed in a river or turned over for rending, just as they always had. To Mr. Winbridge's credit, however, and no doubt in deference to the local police, Topper was allowed to remain, and is there to this very day. In its way, this makes Topper's grave as much a milestone as Cherry's: his headstone stands in memory of a true pioneer, the first mutt to crash the cemetery gates and lie among the elites.

Outside of Britain, meanwhile, animal cemeteries had begun to appear on the Continent. The first was in Berlin, although it did not last long and the details are vague. Situated on a plot of land adjacent to a cemetery in the Treptow district in the city's southeast, it was founded sometime after Hyde Park in the 1880s, and was even more exclusive. The grounds were administered by a man known locally as Hund (or "Dog") Vogel—a fitting name, given that this particular cemetery was specifically restricted to dogs. In addition, burial was permitted only for those that met a specific requirement. They had to be "moral heroes of the breed," meaning that, beyond being pedigreed, they needed to have proven themselves through performing some kind of valorous act, most typically saving the life of a human.[25]

It is perhaps no surprise to learn that the grounds were small. After all, there may not have been many dogs that made the grade. The location near a human cemetery was apparently chosen because many of the owners of these valorous animals had plots there, and Hund Vogel wanted the dogs to be buried as close as possible to the people they had once served. Small tablets above each grave told of the exceptional acts of each dog; most notable were those of a collie, which was said to have saved six adults and nine children from drowning. Unfortunately for the dogs, their heroism was not enough to save their cemetery, which was bulldozed sometime after Hund Vogel died in the 1890s.

A new cemetery soon appeared, however, established by 1901. This burial ground, founded by a veterinary clinic and located on Berlin's north side, was open to non-heroic dogs. Indeed, it even made a point of not discriminating on account of "race, color, or previous condition of servitude," which was apparently the administration's way of saying plebian dogs were allowed.[26] It eventually grew to seven hundred graves surrounded by vines, shrubs, and small trees, while the grave markers featured such inscriptions as, "Here lies my good Rudolph, aged 13 years, my true comrade, my joy and my last good fortune," and, "Here sleeps my little Bobby, the sunshine of the house."

Unfortunately, the city's administration decided an animal cemetery was less important than the expansion of a nearby market, and this burial ground was likewise bulldozed, in the 1920s. Berlin's dogs just couldn't get a break: two more cemeteries failed, and not long after that the Nazis came to power and expressed a vehement distaste for animal burials. "Let other countries do as they like about such stupidity," wrote an editorialist in a party paper, claiming that such sentimentality "is only carried on by old maids and the like. It has nothing to do with the love of dogs. We live in the new Reich, where the child and not the dog is the centre of family life."[27]

At that point, pet cemeteries in Germany were effectively buried until the second half of the century. Those near Berlin were not the only ones to come and go. By 1910, pet cemeteries had popped up all over Europe, from Denmark in the north to Croatia in the south. Brussels had one, as did Amsterdam. Few of these burial grounds lasted long, however. Even the granddaddy of them all, in Mr. Winbridge's garden, could have easily vanished as well had not Hyde Park's administration the foresight to preserve it as a historic monument. But while others fell into obscurity, the greatest of all, in Paris, was built to last.

It was conceived in the late 19th century, when residents of Paris found the problem of providing a loving goodbye to animal companions compounded by a confusing set of decrees issued by the city's government. It was permissible to bury a pet, but the interment had to be on the owner's private land, and at least a hundred yards from a domicile. Considering that most Parisians lived in homes or apartments on small plots in densely packed neighborhoods, this made burial according to the rules theoretically feasible, but in practical terms impossible. Meanwhile, it had been declared illegal to dispose of an animal in a river or trash dump. There were various other nooks and crannies in the statutes, which altogether combined to entangle grieving pet owners in a kind of Gordian knot.

This was the conclusion an attorney named Georges Harmois came to after visiting a local police station to inquire how he might legally dispose of a recently deceased dog. If he couldn't do this, that, or the other, he asked, what *could* he do? The police were vague in their replies. When Harmois pressed them, they acknowledged that, according to the existing regulations, he really couldn't do much with the body at all. He could definitely take it to a taxidermist, however, they at least offered that by way of suggestion if he were intent on following the letter of the law.

Fortunately for Harmois, he didn't have to make any such decision. The dog was imaginary. Active in animal rights circles, Harmois was curious about

Many German graves were lost, but Ciro's survives: a diplomat's pet, he was buried in London.

the legalities of burials in Paris, and whether it was even possible for residents to give deceased pets their last respects. He found that the situation was as dire as he had feared. "We don't care if we are taunted when we shout out loud that the dog's body deserves better than the garbage box or a hole in the sewer," he proclaimed afterward, "but there is no way in Paris to get rid of a dead animal without risking a citation."[28] The situation was an indignity visited on both pets and their owners, and Harmois vowed to do something about it.

A Grand Vision:
Paris Gets a Pet Cemetery

By 1899, Harmois had partnered with Marguerite Durand, the editor of the journal *La Fronde* and a woman well known in the fight for social causes. Together they unveiled plans for the Cimetière des Chiens et Autres Animaux Domestiques, the Cemetery for Dogs and Other Domestic Animals. That it would go on to become the world's most fabled pet cemetery is no mere accident, but rather the result of meticulous planning. This was a far more organized venture than any previous pet cemetery, and the first in which heart was matched by foresight. Harmois and Durand had formed a stock company, the Société Française Anonyme du Cimetière Pour Chiens et Autres Animaux Domestiques, with themselves as statutory directors holding 500 shares each, and public shares for sale at 100 francs.

The enthusiasm was so great that the company ended up raising 350,000 francs, a financial windfall that would give them the liberty to seek out the ideal location. They found it in the Seine itself: a small island to the northwest of central Paris in Asnières, being offered by the Baron de Bosmolet for 70,000 francs. The plot had previously been known as the Île des Ravageurs, or Island of Ravagers, with a reputation for crime and hard living. In recent years, however, it had been transformed by the petit bourgeois into a riverfront picnic area similar to the Île de la Jatte a few kilometers to the west, where Georges Seurat had set his famed painting of a perfect Parisian Sunday afternoon. And when the deed of sale was completed on June 15, 1899, the island was again transformed. The Île des Ravageurs would now become the Île de Chiens, the Island of Dogs, an idyllic necropolis for domestic animals.

Previous pet cemeteries had grown randomly as new burials were added. But Paris would be different, with an architect, Henri Edeline, engaged to lay out a master plan of crisscrossing avenues dotted with fine monuments, which Edeline himself would be responsible for carving. The idea that a pet cemetery could be laid out in advance was revolutionary at the time, but it would allow

France's long history of expertise and elegance in cemetery design to be placed at the service of animals. The new pet cemetery would look something like a miniature version of Père Lachaise or Montmartre, and even be fronted by its own impressive portal, an imposing triple-arched Art Nouveau gate designed by another architect, Eugène Petit.

If anything, the Cimetière des Chiens may have been too well planned. It so exceeded any prior pet cemetery as to make its predecessors seem obscure in comparison. Hyde Park, for instance, was small and walled off in Mr. Winbridge's garden, leaving it unobtrusive. Molesworth, meanwhile, was in a remote location far from London. But the new animal necropolis in Paris was to be larger than all the others combined and located directly on the Seine in a highly visible location. It was impossible to ignore and became a target for criticism even before it opened.

The sexism we have previously noted again rose its head, with the cemetery derided as a product of "hysterical women," "silly women," and "feminine folly."[29] In this case, such charges were no doubt prompted by the involvement of Durand, who was one of France's most outspoken feminists. Once again, the accusations ignored reality: the driving force behind the project was a man, and its early proponents included numerous prominent male politicians, writers, and artists. There were also complaints about animals being buried too well. Better than some humans, it was claimed, a sign that the new animal cemetery had a perverse set of priorities.

Harmois and Durand simply ignored such detractors. But France's Catholic clergy had its own set of issues with the nascent cemetery, and this was a powerful body that would have to be placated. As the guardians of religious orthodoxy, the clergy were worried that there might be a risk of sacrilege if animals were interred with undue ceremony, or if their graves too closely mimicked those of humans. In response, it was agreed that, to avoid replicating a traditional cemetery too closely, the Cimetière des Chiens would prohibit graveside ceremonies and forbid the use of any religious symbols: there would be no crosses or pleas to God on gravestones, a restriction that became tradition and is still enforced.

In truth, the resemblance to a cemetery for humans was merely a facade, dispelled soon after the gate. The first monument a visitor encountered, towering thirty feet high at its apex, appeared as a mountain peak from which a large dog emerges, carrying a child upon its back. Letters in sunken relief below the paws identify the dog: Barry S. Bernard. This was not a grave, as the real Barry had been stuffed upon his death in Switzerland and to this day remains in Bern, at the Natural History Museum. Instead, it was a cenotaph, a false burial site, designed by Edeline to declare the incalculable debt mankind owes to animals by conjuring the image of what at the time was considered history's most heroic dog.

St. Bernards had been named for the remote and dangerous pass in the Swiss Alps, which in turn had been named in honor of St. Bernard of Menthon.

In the 11th century, he had founded a hospice on an 8,000-foot peak in order to aid travelers, and it was there that the big dogs were bred to seek out lost or injured people among the crags of the pass. The gentle giants carried small casks of supplies to aid any they might find, and would lead them back to safety or, if they were injured, return with rescuers.

As a group, the dogs who served the pass were legendary, and Barry was the greatest legend among them. None knew the area like he, and none of them were as tenaciously dedicated to their harrowing task. Starting in 1800, he was credited with saving forty travelers, including a boy trapped on an icy ledge. The child, lost and exhausted, had fallen unconscious from fatigue and was half frozen by the time the dog found him. Using his massive body, Barry warmed the child to revive him, and the boy then climbed onto his back and was carried to the hospice. This is the remarkable story of canine heroism recounted in the sculpture in Paris.

Not only was Barry steadfast in his duty, he sacrificed himself to it, dying in his attempt to rescue traveler number forty-one, in 1812. An injured man, unable to make out the large animal coming at him through the snow and afraid he was about to be set upon by a wolf, fired a fateful shot. Barry fell dead, high up in the frozen Alps, in the very pass he had faithfully patrolled for more than a decade. His death at the hands of his final rescue is recalled in an inscription on his statue in Paris: "He saved the life of 40 people . . . he was killed by the 41st."

Considering Barry's valiant service and tragic end, it is easy to see why the founders of the Cimetière des Chiens chose him as their masthead. Of course, to what extent his story is entirely true is another matter. There had been a lineage of St. Bernards named Barry who patrolled the pass, and it has been suggested that the biographies of several of them had been conflated into a single, mythic dog. In addition, the story of his death during a rescue attempt may be entirely fictive, as other accounts claim he lived out his last years in comfort in Bern after being retired from service due to old age.[30] This is a more likely scenario considering that his body was available in the city and in good enough condition to be stuffed. There are even doubts about whether the story of the child's rescue is true.

Nitpicking the historical record overlooks the true meaning of the statue, however. Larger than life and set at the entrance, it was intended to serve not as a monument to a specific dog, but rather as a symbol of the selfless dedication animals have offered to humanity. Whatever the truth of Barry's story, it was widely believed at the time, so recounting it provided a familiar legend that showed the unity of man and animal. And in Barry's case, the animal was not

Henri Edeline's monumental tribute to Barry still stands at the entrance to the Cimetière des Chiens.

only a faithful servant but also a means of salvation and, in the end, a martyr. The sculpture effectively takes the place of a statue of Christ or a saint at the entrance to a parish cemetery. Moreover, as a statement of purpose it declares that, while this may be a different kind of burial ground, it should nonetheless be considered as much a *terra sancta* as any in which a human might be interred.

The Cimetière des Chiens did such brisk business at the outset that the question of which animal's burial broke ground has become a matter of debate.[31] None was specifically recorded as the first, although some accounts claim the initial interment was for a dog named Tonkin, owned by Juliette Darcourt, a popular actress from the Opéra-Comique and Théatre du Vaudeville. Others say that it was for a mutt named Pompon, who lived among the soldiers at the Camp de Châlons, a military training ground near Paris. Yet another story gives the honor to a dog named Lou Lou, who, at the tender age of nine months, jumped into the Garonne River to save the drowning daughter of her owner. Little Lou Lou broke her leg in the process but emerged a hero. Dying at the young age of five, she was honored with one of the cemetery's notable early monuments, her name in stone encircled by a carved dog's leash, with "Testimonial of gratitude from a mother" inscribed below.

There is an additional account that claims that the first burial was for a dog owned by a young woman who arrived with the body in a small box on the very day the cemetery was opened. She was terribly grieved by the loss, and, as the cemetery was understaffed, a sympathetic accountant working in the office obliged to assist her, making sure that her pet was laid to rest in one of the recently dug graves. Her grief was so inconsolable, however, that he offered to see her home. He did not return to work that day, nor the next. Finally, after his absence continued to stretch over several days, word arrived: the pair had fallen in love and had been wed.

Whichever burial came first, and whether or not it sparked a romance, the floodgates had been opened. The founders proved correct in their assessment of Paris's need for a pet cemetery, and the Cimetière des Chiens quickly became the largest in the world, with an astounding 16,000 burials during its first two decades. And even though the administration had agreed to avoid graveside services, there were still plenty of other trappings. These included a *ceremoniaire*, the cemetery's equivalent of an undertaker, who would call at the owner's home, dressed in black livery, to wrap the animal's body in fine linen and place it in an appropriately sized coffin. It would then be transported to the grounds by an autocycle hearse, a tricycle decked out in black with a cart attached to the front. Mourning cards were prepared to inform the owner's friends of the pet's passing. One surviving example reads, "Madame _____: We have the regret to make known to you the death in his thirteenth year of our faithful, devoted friend, the brave Bijou, who defended his mistress and on one occasion saved her life. He reposes in the Dog Cemetery in Asnières, where anyone may visit his tomb. Think of him."[32]

The early headline attractions were, predictably, pets of famous and high-ranking people, and they represented a who's who of politicians, aristocrats, and celebrities of *fin de siècle* Paris. These burials helped establish the prestige of the new cemetery, and among the prominent names were the French president Félix Faure, who died in office the year the cemetery was opened; Cléo de Mérode, a dancer of the Belle Époque who was considered the first celebrity icon, and the first woman whose photographic image was distributed internationally; the composer Camille Saint-Saëns; Gabrielle Réjane, an actress who so successfully embodied the ideal Parisienne that *Le Figaro* declared her to be the soul of the city; and Sully Prudhomme, the poet and essayist who, in 1901, received the first Nobel Prize in Literature.

And even though the French had deposed their own monarchy over a century before, there was nonetheless no shortage of royal burials. The Russian princess Vera Nikolaievna Lobanov Rostovsky spared no expense in memorializing her dogs Marquise and Tony. She was one of the wealthiest ex-patriots in France, famed for her collection of jewelry, and had the pair honored together on a stone monument sculpted in the round, each of them life-sized and alert, sitting upright upon separate levels. Below them, a lower register is inscribed with their names upon an escutcheon topped by a coronet. Reputed to be the most expensive grave marker in the cemetery, it was whispered to have cost 100,000 francs.

The honor for the most remarked-upon grave, however, fell to a different royal commission, for a greyhound named Emma, owned by Gaëtana Pignatelli

Little more than a bicycle with a box, this hearse was used to pick up dead pets.

À MEMOIRE
de ma chère
EMMA
du 12 AVRIL 1889
au 2 AOÛT 1900
fidèle compagne
et seule amie de ma vie
errante et désolée

di Cerchiara, the blue-blooded black sheep of an aristocratic Neapolitan family. Born to a princess's crown, she had been seduced by the underbelly of Paris, working as a cabaret singer, and was alleged to have been available as a high-level prostitute. Trapped in a wayward existence equally measured in adventure and tragedy, she had come to rely on her dog as her only source of genuine affection. Following Emma's death in 1900, the fallen princess commissioned a stone monument depicting a canopy draped over a recumbent dog's body, surmounted by a crown as a reminder of her own birthright. But the grave marker proved as famous for its inscription as for the quality of the sculpture. It reads, "To the memory of my dog Emma, faithful companion and the only friend of my wandering and desolate life."

Not all the notable early burials were for dogs, however. Unlike Hyde Park and Molesworth, which were listed as dog cemeteries even though they accommodated other species, the burial ground in Paris specifically included in its title "and other domestic animals." Those words were no mere appendage, as the founders included quarters dedicated to cats, birds, and miscellaneous types within the original design. Cats in particular had a visibility they had

Gaëtana Pignatelli's tribute to Emma featured a sculpted portrait of the dog on its deathbed.

A memorial to infantry mascot Memere and the grave of Marquise and Tony highlight the grounds.

not attained elsewhere, with sculptures of domestic felines placed throughout the grounds. And on the larger end of the feline spectrum, the Cimetière des Chiens hosted the first ever grave in a pet cemetery for a lion, by the name of Mine.

One of the most touching early burials, meanwhile, was for a goldfinch named Gazouille. While the grave itself was not grand, the story behind it is. A pair of children, Paul and Jeanne, had rescued the bird from a cruel man who had tortured her and put out her eyes. It was the children who gave her the name Gazouille, the word meaning "chirp." Her injuries had already sealed her fate, but they treated her with tenderness and gave her all the love they could in the time she had left. After the bird's passing, a grave was provided as a gift of the cemetery, and the children, who had become heroes to Paris's animal lovers, buried her with their own hands.

The Cimetière des Chiens was also more democratic than its predecessors in another important respect. Despite all its grandiosity, burials were decidedly not the province of elites alone, as the administration had taken into account the city's poor by including a potter's field for pets. This was a common plot where people of lesser means could inter their companion animals—in

effect, the Toppers of the world—with dignity and without controversy. The graves were allowed to remain for three to five years before they were removed to free up room for others.

This was not a sign of disrespect, however. All burials were considered to be on leased ground unless a financial arrangement had been made to preserve them in perpetuity, a practice intended to optimize space and ensure income for the maintenance of the property. Unfortunately, it resulted in many of the

early graves being later removed, and today many of the most notable burials are known only through photographs. Of the paupers' burials, which never received more than small wooden markers, nothing at all is preserved. Some of their inscriptions were recorded, however, including one that bore a quote attributed to the mathematician and philosopher Blaise Pascal: "The more that I see of men, the more I prefer dogs."[33]

Still among the world's foremost resting places for animals, the Cimetière des Chiens et Autres Animaux Domestiques has by now hosted over 60,000 burials. But the desire that the cemetery should serve the dignity of those animals who lived far from the lap of luxury has never been abandoned, and it resonates even in some of the cemetery's most important grave markers. There is one dated to 1958, for instance—a stone plaque commemorating the 40,000th interment. This milestone was not reserved for some noble or famous creature, but was given in charity to a stray dog that lived nearby and died at the cemetery's gate. He may have lacked a home during his life, but he was provided one in eternity.

The cemetery's dedication to the city's most humble animals has also carried over into the 21st century. In 2013, for example, a grave was dedicated to 100 cats from a nearby rescue whose deaths spanned nearly two decades.

Vintage images: a trolley passing the cemetery gates, a view from above, and visitors to the graves.

OVERLEAF: *Among the charitable graves is one for the cremated remains of rescue cats from Asnières.*

ICI REPOSENT 100 CHATS
DE L'ASSOCIATION DES AMIS
DES CHATS D'ASNIÈRES

La prière du chat

L'être que je suis n'a pas de maître,
Mais un ami que je choisis,
Sans qui je peux mourir d'ennui.

Respecte mon indépendance,
Je te prouverai, librement, en caresses,
Et "ron ron" que je t'aime.

Traite moi donc en égal,
Je ne suis pas ta peluche !

Et s'il le faut, des années,
Je t'attendrai, mon ami...

Their cremated remains are buried under a headstone featuring a collage of their photos and these words in tribute:

A Cat's Prayer

I am a creature that has no master
But rather a friend of my choosing,
Without whom I would die of boredom.
Respect my independence,
And I shall repay you freely with caresses,
And mews that say I love you.
Treat me as an equal,
For I am not a toy!,
And no matter how long it takes,
I will wait for you, my friend . . .

George Harmois and Marguerite Durand would be proud of their creation. Other burial grounds came and went, and some were lost entirely. But the Cimetière des Chiens carries on well into its second century, the great survivor of the first wave of pet cemeteries in Europe, a product of a vision that insisted animals be remembered with respect and dignity. That vision was seen on the other side of the Atlantic as well. Even while the Cimetière des Chiens was still in its infancy, an even bigger wave was set to crash that shore, as the Americans were already hard at work constructing what would become the world's largest network of pet cemeteries.

OVERLEAF: *More vintage images, graves, and a girl paying tribute. The inscription dedicated to Sapho was once famous for the dog's owner vowing to forgo Heaven if they were not allowed entry together.*

MA NINI CHÉRIE
TU FUS LES ONZE ANNÉES DE TA VIE
MA SEULE CONSOLATION
MES LARMES
NE TARIRONT QU'A M... ORT
DEUX AOUT 193...
L. HÉNO...

CONCESSION DIX ANS

SAPHO et DJERID
amis de Tola Dorian

Je l'on Aime, Sapho, n'accompagne la mienne,
O chère et noble amie, aux ignorés séjours,
Je ne veux pas du Ciel! Je veux, quoiqu'il advienne
M'endormir comme Toi, sans réveil, pour toujours.

7 octobre 1901

PRÈS DE CETTE TOMBE
MARCHEZ SANS FAIRE DE BRUIT
GILLETTE MON TRÉSOR
N'EST PAS MORTE
MAIS ELLE DORT
DEPUIS LE 5 FÉVRIER 1921
AGÉE DE 11 ANS
SA MÈRE ÉPLORÉE
B. G.

II

Brave New World
Early Pet Cemeteries in the United States

II

 New Women and Dead Dogs:
The Founding of an Industry

It remains one of the most curious cases in the history of American animal burials. In 1926, a Gordon setter named Clipper from Boonton, New Jersey, was getting on in years and had shown definite signs of illness. Naturally, this was of great concern to his human family, that of Mr. and Mrs. Raymond Zeek. To their relief, however, the old boy demonstrated a new verve one morning. In a sudden flourish of activity, he wandered out into the backyard and began digging a hole. Perhaps he was not so sick after all. In fact, the exact opposite was true. They left him to his devices, only to return an hour later to find a rectangular trench two feet deep and exactly the length of Clipper's body— with him lying dead beside it. The dog had dug his own grave, and while the family was as flummoxed as they were heartbroken, there was nothing to do but bury him. When asked about the incident, the Zeeks were at a loss for an explanation, other than to remark that Clipper had always been "a smart dog."[1]

Perhaps so, but not smart enough to know that he could have saved himself the effort. By the time of Clipper's death, the United States was well on its way to creating a network of over 600 pet cemeteries. No one has ever taken to the task like the Americans, who have built more pet cemeteries than the rest of the world combined. They are found from sea to shining sea, in every conceivable terrain and in an astounding variety of types. There are New Age-styled burial grounds where wind chimes ring out over the graves like hidden voices, desolate graveyards devoted to pets owned by RVers, and cemeteries specifically for police dogs. A cemetery even exists solely for coon dogs—no other country even recognizes these raccoon-hunting hounds as a breed, but the United States has an entire cemetery dedicated to them. Pet cemeteries are as American as baseball and apple pie.

But it hasn't always been that way. In the mid to late 19th century, the situation in American cities was fundamentally no different than in Europe, with dead pets handed over for rending or thrown into rivers, and many people scrambling for surreptitious solutions. In fact, if anything, the plight in many American towns was worse. There was already a network of what were called "dog cemeteries," but the term had a very different meaning in the United States, referring to dumping grounds. At the time, stray dogs roamed in large packs, and to prevent them from attacking people they would be hunted down and shot in coordinated campaigns. A "dog cemetery" would then be designated as a place to dispose of them, and dead pets could be taken there as well.[2] It must have been utterly ghastly to see one's pet tossed among the rotting

bodies of strays, but it was reported that some grieving owners braved the horror to build small memorials.

Americans did have certain advantages, however, since the United States was a huge country with vast expanses of scarcely populated land. As in England, people with estates might establish their own private cemeteries. The most prominent example was that of John Tyler, the country's tenth president, who kept a veritable zoo at his rural Virginia residence, and various dogs, cats, and horses were buried in a cemetery that is still maintained by his descendants. The United States had something in addition, however: the frontier, and people living there could bury animals as they pleased. And many did. There are numerous accounts attesting to graves for especially dogs, although scant records were kept of the locations of even human burials, and of animals not at all.

In one case, however, a dog's grave made his owners rich. In 1874, two men were out hunting deer near Moose Lake, Montana, when one accidentally discharged his gun, killing their dog Towser. The men agreed to give him a decent burial, and in the process of digging a grave they discovered some interesting-looking rocks. An assayer confirmed they were rich in high-grade copper, and a mine was founded. As for Towser, he was buried as planned, although his peace was disturbed twenty-four years later when laborers breaking ground

Visitors to the now-lost pet cemetery in Washington, D.C., in the early 20th century.

OVERLEAF: *Diversity ranges from hunting-dog cemeteries to the New Age beauty of Angel's Rest in Utah.*

on a new shaft accidentally unearthed his skeleton.[3]

However many dogs were buried on the frontier, only one grave can still be positively identified, that of Thornburgh, at Fort Bridger, Wyoming. He was discovered as a pup in 1879, yelping at the side of his dead mother in the aftermath of a battle. Taken by soldiers, he wound up living at Fort Bridger, where he made a name for himself by catching a thief attempting to rob the commissary. The man had already filled his bags when Thornburgh jumped him. In the ensuing melee, the dog suffered a slash from a knife along his side, but the intruder got worse, as he was badly mauled. Thornburgh would go on to prove his bravery several more times, and when he died in 1888 the soldiers gave him not just a grave, but a headstone with an inscription that could not be more fitting for a frontier dog: "Sleep on, old fellow, we'll meet across the range."

Back in the big cities of the East Coast, however, burials had to be kept on the down low, and a brisk trade quietly developed among morticians willing to provide services to pet owners. One acknowledged this in 1883 when a reporter visited his funeral parlor to inquire about a dog named Rover who had been owned by a young girl from a wealthy Chicago family. While they were visiting New York, the poor pooch had been struck by a coach on Broadway and killed, and the girl's grief was such that her parents promised that the dog would receive an honorable burial.

THORNBURGH
DIED
SEPT 27, 1888

Man never had a better, truer, braver friend. Sleep on old fellow. We'll meet across the Range.

A photo believed to include Thornburgh, among friends from Fort Bridger who later laid him to rest.

President Tyler himself penned the epitaph placed over the grave of his favorite horse, General.

Epitaph for President Tyler's favorite horse buried in the grove at Sherwood Forest.

Here lie the bones of my old horse, "General,"
Who served his master faithfully
for twenty-one years,
And never made a blunder.
Would that his master could say the same!

Word on the street was that the mortician had been hired to embalm Rover and construct a glass-topped mahogany casket. "Don't say anything about it," the mortician beseeched the reporter, although he did admit that he had been similarly preparing several dozen pets a year.[4]

Exactly what the owners were doing with these animals remains a mystery, save for the few cases in which it was inadvertently revealed, such as that of a cat owned by Mrs. Peter Adams of Madison Avenue, New York, in the 1890s. A member of the Long Island Country Club in Eastport, she had the body of her purebred Angora prepared by a mortician and sent to the club for burial. This was much to the surprise of the superintendent, who had not been advised in advance. He received a package from her one day and found inside a small coffin containing the dead cat, along with a note explaining that, since the club had plenty of open space, Mrs. Adams hoped he could do her the favor of finding a shady nook to bury her pet.[5]

American pet owners also proved far more determined than their European counterparts to inter their animals in human cemeteries. In the United States, the popular strategy was to sneak pets in, and since the true measure of a secret act is that it remains secret, we can never know how many people succeeded. Tantalizing hints periodically reveal that the number may be high, however, such as a locked metal box that came open after the better part of a century in the mausoleum of Dr. Clark Dunlop at Woodlawn Cemetery in the Bronx. Providing a shock for a maintenance worker, it contained the skeleton of a large parrot.

But many attempts also failed, resulting in decades' worth of tragicomic scandals. Highlights include an episode in Illinois in which a group of cemetery plot holders banded together under the threat of removing their human relatives to another burial ground in order to force the exhumation of a pet from another family's plot. In Missouri, the exact opposite occurred when an oil magnate had his family exhumed and reburied elsewhere—and a $10,000 bequest in his will intended for the cemetery cancelled—when his dog's grave was discovered and orders were given that its body be disinterred. Meanwhile, in Los Angeles, an attempt by a widow to bury her husband's dog alongside him resulted in a court hearing in which her mental competence was put on trial.[6]

The "classic" case of this kind in the United States involved a Skye terrier named Cosey, owned by Mary Bell, a widow from New York, who in 1888 laid the dog to rest at Woodlawn Cemetery. Cosey had died on August 12, and Mary engaged an undertaker to prepare him for burial while she made arrangements. She was diligent, and specifically wanted to avoid subterfuge when interring her pet. Before purchasing a plot, therefore, she carefully checked the cemetery's rules. They stated only that the grounds were for the burial of the dead, with no mention of species. She then inquired at the city offices as to whether a certificate of some kind was needed for the burial of a dog. Technically no, she was told, since death and burial certificates for dogs didn't exist.

Confident that she was in the clear, Mary had Cosey's body combed and perfumed, placed in a child's coffin trimmed in purple velvet and blue satin, and delivered to the cemetery. A eulogy was read as Mary and a handful of friends said their final goodbyes, and the grave was marked with a marble sarcophagus. Things had gone well. Too well, as it turned out: when news of the burial spread, a sudden outcry came from Woodlawn's other plot holders. The ensuing scandal had legs, far longer than a Skye terrier's, and the story was reported to an aghast audience.

Both Mary and Cosey were attacked with such vitriol that one might think the burial had been an act of treason. One of the "most disgusting incidents of the present year was the recent 'funeral' of a wretched Skye terrier owned by a person—she can hardly be called a lady and certainly not a woman—named Mrs. Mary A. Bell,"[7] wrote one angry editorialist, who also piled shame upon Mary for spending an estimated five hundred dollars on a dog's funeral while poor children and orphans went without food. Of course, countless funerals for wealthy people were held daily around the country at a much greater cost, but the author had no complaints about those, the blame for the suffering of these poor urchins being laid squarely on Cosey's now cold nose.

The cemetery's administration also came under fire for permitting "such a beastly and offensive spectacle."[8] In fact, Woodlawn's president and vice president

"Burying the Dog" by Randolph Caldecott, who was born in England but died in Florida in 1886.

had no idea that Cosey had been buried there, both having been away at the time, and they were none too happy about it. The onslaught of negative press brought considerable pressure on them to act. They told Mary in no uncertain terms that Cosey had to go and that, if she did not exhume him, they would. Despite Mary's careful preparations, Cosey was forced out, removed to a private burial site with the details undisclosed. As for the rules, they were changed to clearly specify that only *human* dead were permitted in Woodlawn.

The scandal involving Cosey Bell at least had the effect of bringing to the public's attention the need for a pet cemetery in New York. A topic of much discussion by the 1890s, the matter was pressed by a woman who, while declining to be publicly identified, spoke eloquently on the subject with a newspaper reporter in 1896. "Do we not read every day in the papers . . . of pet dogs who are put away in expensive caskets, but for whom there is no resting place in the cemeteries devoted to men?," she asked. Answering her own question, she explained how a pet owner who "is sincerely attached to a dog is as anxious that he should have decent burial or disposition after death as if it were a case of a child."[9]

This mystery woman was not simply speculating on the need for such a burial ground. She was also preparing to establish one, her dream being an American animal necropolis that would set the standard for the rest of the world. The article even carried an illustration of what she proposed, looking remarkably like the Cimetière des Chiens, which was itself still only a dream another three years in the making. While this woman was never publicly identified, there can be no doubt that she was Emily Berthet. The forgotten visionary of the American pet cemetery industry, her name has for over a century been curiously absent from its founding in favor of a story involving a prominent New York veterinarian who was asked by a grieving woman if he could recommend a place to bury her dog. He offered his apple orchard in Hartsdale, twenty-five miles from New York City, and from this act of kindness a cemetery was soon born.[10]

The veterinarian was real—his name was Dr. Samuel Johnson—but he owned no apple orchard. Instead, it was Emily who owned property in Hartsdale, and she had begun burying pets there by 1898. This is clear from the first press reports on what would become Hartsdale Pet Cemetery, still active today after a hundred thousand burials, which gave all the credit to her and did not even mention Dr. Johnson's name. So why did the revised history later take hold? Emily was what they called at the time a "new woman," strong-willed and independent. That in itself was not the blackest of marks, but her reputation was especially dubious because she had been living openly in a romantic relationship with a married man.[11] On his death, a battle with his estranged wife ensued. Yet he had deeded the property in Hartsdale to Emily, and it was hers to do with as she chose.

What she chose was to found the country's first pet cemetery. But even Emily must have realized that she was not the best person to front a new

enterprise in late 19th-century America. This is probably why she chose to keep her name out of the 1896 article. In addition, she needed contacts to spread the word among the pet-loving community. Dr. Johnson was a professor of veterinary surgery at New York University and active in the American Society for the Prevention of Cruelty to Animals. With a stellar reputation in the animal welfare world, he could provide such contacts. Whether Emily approached him or vice versa is unknown, but they soon partnered on the pet cemetery, and for public consumption it became Dr. Johnson's.

And eventually it was. But not until 1913, when he bought the property outright. Having partnered on the venture before spending the rest of his life tending the only rival to the Cimetière des Chiens in terms of longevity and history, Samuel Johnson rightly earned his place as the father of the American pet cemetery industry. As for its mother, however, she died the year she finally ceded ownership, and without even a whispered reminder of her role. Whatever happened behind the scenes, whether it was a soap opera of intrigue that pushed her out, or whether the decisions made were amicable, we have no clue, although Emily never publicly expressed bitterness over being erased from her creation.

That was all still to come when the first pets were laid to rest, however. By October 1898, there were scarcely more than a dozen graves, and the venture was so new that there weren't even any permanent headstones, just wooden shingles on poles indicating plot numbers. But stonecutters were at work on the grave markers, plots were on sale to the general public, a sexton had been hired, and a plan was in place for continued expansion across a three-acre parcel. Dr. Johnson had begun spreading the word, and an agent was in place in New York to help organize transport for pets' bodies. The dream was becoming a reality, and on October 16 the *New York Sun* carried the news back to the city under the headline, "New York Now Has a Place to Bury Its Dead Pets."[12]

 ## *Hartsdale:*
America Reinvents the Pet Cemetery

With the grounds devoid of monuments, the focus in the early days at Hartsdale was on the animals themselves. The biggest star, thanks to the lavishness of both his life and his funeral, was a spaniel named Major. Owned by Mrs. John T. Stephens, a wealthy widow, he was one of the most valuable dogs in the country,

A woman, believed to be a Belgian immigrant named Helen Farenholtz, leaves flowers at a grave at Hartsdale.

claimed to be worth $1,500—an amount so large it was said to be a "sum [for which] anyone could buy a hundred babies or more from their parents in New York."[13] And Major had tastes to match his price tag. These included a peculiar affinity for good coffee. Each morning, a freshly brewed pot would be brought up to his bedroom by a liveried servant. The dog's manners were so refined that he would not drink it until a bib was tied under his chin, and when he was finished he would offer his snout to be wiped.

Despite this, Major was not complacent. Always vigilant towards the humans around him, he had saved a child from drowning in Georgia, a feat that had earned him a medal, and had later saved two more children at Rockaway Beach. He could even talk, as well as sing in three different languages—at least according to Mrs. Stephens, who realized such claims might push the bounds of credibility and was quick to offer the caveat that *she* could understand him, even if no one else did. Major's end came at age eleven, after contracting inflammation of the lungs. As he lay dying, he was serenaded with the Greater Doxology, "Gloria in excelsis Deo," which Mrs. Stephens asserted he was particularly fond of. He was then adorned in a golden collar and buried in a glass-topped rosewood casket, with the Doxology sung again as he was lowered into the ground.

Hartsdale grew rapidly over the next few years. In 1905, the *New York Times* visited the spot "where all good New York dogs go" when they die, and reported that the orchard had begun to look like an authentic rural cemetery.[14] Many small stone grave markers and some more elaborate ones had by then been installed, and there was an average of around fifteen new burials a month, a number that was supplemented by people exhuming their pets from other sites for reburial at Hartsdale as a safe, permanent resting place. The grounds were a joy to the senses, so overgrown with flowers that it was as if "the begonia had been voted the favorite flower of the spirits of departed little barking dogs," and the walkways were lined with pink and white roses, hemlock, and orange-flowered lilacs.[15] Bird feeders and bowls of seed brought in tanagers, orioles, sparrows, and robins.

Hartsdale was then titled a canine cemetery, but the dogs had to "share it with a few of the cats [they] have chased in life."[16] Feline burials were mostly confined to an area along the back fence, although the cats were hardly second-class citizens—especially not Mignon, another of the early stars. Owned by the socialite Ada Van Tassel Billington, Mignon was worth more than three hundred dollars, an unheard-of amount for a cat in those days, and her grave was considered the nicest in the cemetery. Surrounded by boxed shrubs and two flower gardens, it was the only plot with its own private groundskeeper, a gardener from Woodlawn Cemetery who had been hired to make regular trips up from the Bronx to tend it.

Over the next decade, more tracts of land were acquired, spruce and maple trees planted, a full-time caretaker hired, and a cottage built as an office.

The rapid growth was necessary to keep up with an exponential increase in burials. A 1917 report noted that in the past three years there had been more burials than in the preceding eighteen combined, and that the requests for plots in the first eight months of 1917 were already double those of the year before. By that time, in the twenty-one years since the cemetery's founding, there had been 2,000 burials. Three years later the total was up to 3,000, and within the next decade the number had tripled. Pet burials had become big business.

There were of course detractors. The types of people who blamed the plight of starving orphans on Cosey Bell's funeral found plenty of reasons to complain about the expense of memorializing pets at Hartsdale. There were critics especially among the locals, who derisively referred to the grounds as the "mutt orchard."[17] They even managed to lodge the most bizarre complaint ever made against a pet cemetery, telling a reporter from nearby Mt. Vernon that their own dogs were disappearing as a result of conflicts with canine ghosts that would rise from the graves and "stalk about at night to frighten the village mongrels."[18] But no one else was concerned with the phantoms—or at least not until Stephen King—and even people who didn't care for pets found the

The shrubs and flower gardens that once surrounded Mignon's grave are gone, but the stone remains.

Hartsdale's early highlights included this grave with a delicately rendered carving of a dog named Babe.

cemetery more fascinating than offensive. During the summer, there might be a log jam of cars on the narrow road that led to the gates as curiosity seekers came to tour the grounds, read the stones, and be touched by the alternately earnest and wacky sentiment on display.

Undoubtedly the biggest story on the grounds was Goldfleck, a star-crossed lion who had been owned by a Hungarian princess, Elisabeth Vilma Lwoff-Parlaghy. She had earned her royal status by wedding a Russian prince, and even though their marriage was short-lived she kept the title when she emigrated to the United States in 1908. In tow was what amounted to a small zoo, including ibises, owls, alligators, and a bear. This retinue, along with her collection of art and antiques, was installed in a fourteen-room suite in the Plaza Hotel. From the sound of it, she already had everything she could possibly need—and much that she didn't—but in 1911 her love of excess was lured by something she couldn't have. While visiting the Barnum & Bailey circus at Madison Square Garden, she fell madly in love with a lion cub.

The fact that the circus refused to sell him probably only made the princess want him all the more. Favors were called in from a powerful friend, Daniel Sickles, a former Civil War general who had himself been the subject of controversy when he attempted to bury his dog Bobo in his family's cemetery plot in New Rochelle, New York. With the general as the princess's advocate, the six-week-old cub was sold for $250, an acquisition that turned out to be the worst thing that could have possibly happened to the lion. Goldfleck survived the princess for just over a year. He spent the summer with her in Europe, and upon his return, being no longer a cub, the hotel asked that he be moved to Bronx Zoo. But the princess once again got her way, and he would spend the rest of his days at the Plaza, save for occasional walks on a leash in Central Park and an incident in which he escaped into a hallway and had to be lured back with raw meat.

Effectively a leonine Rapunzel trapped in a luxury hotel, Goldfleck eventually succumbed to a case of gout brought on by a wildly inappropriate diet. A wake was held at the Plaza, with his body covered in wreaths and flowers, and in a procession of six cars of mourners he was taken to Hartsdale, to finally be freed from his captivity. The headstone honoring the noble beast that fell victim to a wealthy woman's flight of fancy is still one of the most popular in the cemetery. Located near the top of the rolling hill that leads down from the gate, it reads, "Beneath this stone is buried the beautiful young lion Goldfleck whose death was sincerely mourned by his mistress, Princess Lwoff Parlaghy. New York 1912."

The story of the little lion who never had a chance was heartbreaking, but anyone who needed a pick-me-up merely had to stroll over to the grave

Goldfleck's mistress provided only a simple headstone,
with the lion added by later admirers.

of Grumpy the Bulldog. In fact, it couldn't be missed: measuring well over six feet high, it was the tallest monument on the grounds, a thin spire carved to a point at the top. In the upper half, between the words "Our loved one" and Grumpy's name, was a huge bronze medallion cast in the image of his face, as if a portal had opened in the stone and he was emerging in some transcendent and immutable form. The lower section carried the epitaph, "His sympathetic love and understanding enriched our lives. He waits for us." The marker towered over the nearby gravestones with the imposing presence of an ancient Akkadian stele, and a visitor would no doubt have wondered what fantastically expensive beast could possibly rest under such a structure.

And the answer was: none. Grumpy wasn't expensive at all, and to his owners—a banker named Henry Bizallion and his wife, Emma—that was the entire point. The Bizallions were among the founders of the Dog Lovers' Protective Association of America, a group for "people who keep dogs for their own sakes rather than their value as exhibitions." Or "jes' dogs," as the organization called everyday canines.[19] Entirely lacking in blue blood and red ribbons, Grumpy was simply a good ol' bulldog of dubious lineage; one suspects he probably wasn't all that grumpy either. On his death, the Bizallions decided there was no reason an ordinary dog didn't deserve as grand a send-off as a medal winner. Or in Grumpy's case, grander. It was a sentiment that any common pet owner could understand. Back in London, Topper would have no doubt been pleased.

Another favorite character was the only dog in the world known to have had an apartment complex named after him. Standing at 2500 University Avenue in the Bronx, the five-story brick building was dubbed the Rex Moore by William M. Moore, a real-estate developer who had honored his St. Bernard as its namesake. And in case his tenants failed to get the reference, he also placed a larger-than-life stone sculpture inscribed with the dog's name above the building's entrance, as well as a painted portrait of Rex in the lobby. The dog's final real-estate holding was, of course, at Hartsdale, where he was buried under a thick stone bearing the epitaph, "Died at his post, July 30, 1919 / Age 7 Years / Always a most faithful and loyal friend / To his master." And loyal not just to his master—he was protective enough of the building bearing his name that he once barked out an alarm to alert tenants of a fire on the property.[20]

Stories about Hartsdale tended to become exaggerated in the telling, which made them all the more interesting. There is, for example, a large mausoleum dedicated in 1917 to Sally and Toodles by Mrs. M. F. Walsh, the widow of a Mt. Vernon real-estate broker. The most prominent monument on the grounds, it was carved from Barre granite, weighed more than fifty tons, and looked

Eventually cut in two—a visible line is seen above the epitaph—Grumpy's gravestone has been restored.

OVERLEAF: *The massive Walsh mausoleum remains the most impressive monument on the grounds.*

something like a pagan temple for munchkins. Of course, it was outlandishly expensive—$13,000 according to the *New York Herald*, which published the first photo of it in 1919.[21] Without doubt, it was the costliest funerary monument ever dedicated to animals in the United States. But as if the original expenditure were not enough, the reported cost was quickly bumped up, to $25,000 and then to $40,000. Meanwhile, the original accounts described it as being "larger than the sarcophagi of the pharaohs," but it was apparently growing as well, and by 1928 it was as large as King Tut's tomb.[22]

Meanwhile, Goldfleck's headstone was inflated to a cost of $13,000, or the price of the entire Walsh mausoleum.[23] While no receipt for its purchase survives, it can be safely said that even though Princess Lwoff-Parlaghy was known to spend lavishly, one thing she didn't break the bank for was her lion's grave marker. It is of only average size, with simple chiseled letters in sunken relief, and the sculpted lion that now stands beside it was not originally there. Goldfleck's grave marker wouldn't come close to costing $13,000 even now. But this level of hyperbole provides an insight into the extent to which Hartsdale was becoming legendary. Americans had embraced the grounds as something more than just a cemetery. It was an exuberant age, one that saw the United States for the first time begin to flex its wealth and power on the world's stage, and in all its weird glory, Hartsdale had come to represent a celebration of the nation's pets.

Not that it was the only place to lay a pet to rest by then. New York had no shortage of entrepreneurs wanting to bury them, and the first headstones were scarcely in place at Hartsdale before another cemetery was announced, in 1899, by a male virility specialist named Dr. H. H. Kane. Best known for newspaper ads carrying testimonials from customers declaring "Made a Man of Me," Kane's greatest interest was in racehorses and dogs, and the private animal cemetery at his Long Island residence was well known among pet enthusiasts. A public version even closer to the city than Hartsdale could be a winner, and he printed up pamphlets detailing the venture.[24] The virility doctor's plan went limp, however, when he couldn't find enough backers at a minimum stake of $1,000, and the *coup de grâce* came when his own wife opted to bury her own dog, King Victor, at Hartsdale in 1904. Thanks to a large headstone that Mrs. Kane kept constantly supplied with flowers, the grave became one of the most prominent on the grounds, and a photo exists of her kneeling beside it.

One pet cemetery that did go forward was Kanis Ruhe, the name being Latin for "Dog's Rest," opened in 1906 by veterinarian Dr. H. K. Miller, owner of the New York Dog and Cat Hospital and president of the New York Cat Club. It was located in Yorktown Heights on a farm that Miller had previously used as a "home for weary animals"—a retirement home apparently, or, as he described it, a place to "pension your faithful horse and dog."[25] Operating as the New York Animal Cemetery Company, Kanis Ruhe became the first pet cemetery in the

United States to be incorporated, and with its location providing easy access to the heart of New York City, it quickly became a popular alternative. According to a 1914 article, within less than a decade it was already one of the largest animal cemeteries in the world, with some two thousand tombstones to be seen. The facility even owned a set of miniature hearses and carriages for mourners, and boasted of onsite embalming, casket manufacturing, and a stone works.

It was at Kanis Ruhe that the most coddled dog in New York was buried: Sport, whose nine years, three months, and sixteen days were spent almost entirely at the side of his owner, Maxine Elliott, the most popular Broadway actress of the era. The only time they weren't together was when she was on stage, but even then Sport wasn't far behind, since he had access to the backstage areas and dressing rooms of any theater in which Elliott performed. And when she opened her own playhouse, it was pretty much his too, as he had free run of the place. The little brindled bulldog even had a special pass allowing him to share his mistress's compartment on Pullman coaches, despite strict railroad regulations to the contrary. Naturally, he would also stay in her hotel rooms, and if the staff was steadfast in enforcing rules against pets, such as in a much-publicized incident at the King Edward Hotel in Toronto, Elliott would let them know what she thought in no uncertain terms and find other lodgings.

When Sport died in 1910, he was given a full funeral service and interred under a marble column costing $3,000 and inscribed, "Sacred to the memory of Sport." It was a headline-grabbing price to pay for a pet's grave marker, but Sport's was only one of many notable early burials at Kanis Ruhe. There was also a grave for a St. Bernard named Rex, owned by state senator James Frawley and descended from none other than the famed Barry. Or at least that was the claim. Whether or not it was true, Rex did share Barry's disposition for serving as a dedicated guide. Each morning he would accompany Frawley's sister to a local elementary school where she was vice principal, and each afternoon he would make his way back to escort her home. The real story, however, was Rex's price tag. The massive dog—a coffin over six feet long had to be built to hold his body—was said to have been worth $5,000.

Maxine Elliott was frequently photographed with Sport, and his burial provided prestige to Kanis Ruhe.

OVERLEAF: *This advertisement for Kanis Ruhe ran in 1909 in the magazine* Country Life in America.

Kanis Ruhe differed from other early pet cemeteries, however, in that the spotlight fell less on lavish burials than on the simple bond that existed between everyday people and their animals. This was due to the unique personality of the cemetery's gravedigger, Barney Davis. It was Davis who showed visitors around, and he had a noted preference for the pets of paupers. Dismissive of the wealthy, he was of the opinion that the death of a pet was harder on the poor than the rich. An animal companion meant more to a person of limited means, Davis believed, and they were therefore more apt to mourn the loss.

"It's not the rich who love their pets," he explained, "it's the poor man, who shares their privations along with them and gets to have a feeling of brotherhood."[26] His favorites among the more pedestrian members of the grounds included a terrier named Jim, who had saved the life of his owner's daughter when a boat overturned in Long Island Sound. Jim had grabbed the hem of the girl's dress with his mouth and pulled her back to shore, and then jumped back into the water to save a boy but became tangled in the boat's rope and was pulled under and drowned. The family was of no great means, yet they made a monthly trip to Yorktown Heights to pay their respects at a hero's grave.

To further make his point, Davis noted a grave marker that was not even inscribed with a name, only the dates 1910–1912. It was for a mutt owned by a tenement family, and the dog had been hit by a truck and killed during the Christmas holidays. "It broke them all up," Davis recalled. By adding all the money that had been set aside for Christmas presents to the mother's meager savings, the family was able to cobble together just enough to afford a grave.[27] Together they followed the dog's body up to Yorktown Heights, having cancelled Christmas in order to provide their dog with a burial. Davis's favorite grave, however, was for a terrier buried by a young woman from the city. She was likewise of limited means, but the haunting epitaph, composed by the owner herself, was priceless: "When the wind mourns on wild winter nights I will think of the comfort you were—perhaps the comfort we were to each other—in those days when each was the only friend the other had."[28]

Westward Ho!:
Pet Cemeteries from Coast to Coast

"'Buried like a dog' is no longer a synonym for indifference and indignity," a reporter was able to declare by the first decade of the 20th century.[29] And it was true. Pet cemeteries were popping up like clover in a field. A fundamental difference between the United States and the rest of the world was the rapidity of the development of its network of animal burial grounds. In England, Molesworth opened only after it was clear Hyde Park would not be able to continue taking more pets, and even now there are still relatively few pet cemeteries. In France, the Cimetière des Chiens was not only the first, it effectively remains *the* pet cemetery for the entire country, as to this day there are only a handful of others. To the north, Canada did not open its first, Happy Woodland, in Aurora, Ontario, until 1933, while to the south, pet cemeteries in Mexico are only now becoming common.

But in the United States people began building them early on and never stopped. Upstate New York had its first by 1901, in the town of Coxsackie.[30] It sounded like a promising venture, funded to a claimed $80,000, although it wound up failing for reasons not recorded. Failure was not unusual among early American pet cemeteries, and in most countries that might dissuade the next potential entrepreneur. In the United States, however, it seemed to matter not one whit. Upstate New York would soon get more, including one that was opened in 1907 and stuck around, founded in the town of Hornell by Frank Myers. Initially, all Myers wanted was a spot to bury his Skye terrier, Trixie, but his request to bury her in his family's plot was predictably denied. Knowing he was not the only person who would face such a predicament, he purchased ten acres of oak and maple groves, and cleared enough land to bury not just his own pet, but those of the community at large.

He named the new cemetery Friendship Grove. Plots there were given away free, with Myers asking only that anyone who buried an animal keep the grave in good order, so as to maintain the overall appearance of the property. The centerpiece of the grounds was Trixie's burial place, marked by a stone column with a descending dove at the top. Myers later interred his favorite St. Bernard nearby, under a marble slab inscribed with excerpts from George Vest's oration for Drum. Many of the other early graves were marked not with stones but with painted tin signs that seem to have been a local specialty. The cemetery was taken over by the Steuben County Humane Society after Myers's death in 1937, and, in a bit of *déjà vu*, the first burial under the new administration mirrored that of the old: it was Myers's own last dog, which had died the day after the passing of his master, the claimed cause being grief.

Friendship Grove is one of the oldest continually operating pet cemeteries in the United States. Yet with its remote location, about seventy-five miles from Rochester as the closest urban center, it averaged only about ten burials a year during its first two decades, and has probably never exceeded a thousand interments. Back in New York City, however, another would open in 1915, on Long Island, and go on to be among the biggest in the world. Founded by Bideawee, the first American no-kill animal shelter, the original burial ground at Wantagh proved so popular that a second was later added in Westhampton. Together, they contain an estimated 65,000 interments.

As at Friendship Grove, the oldest inscribed stone at the Bideawee cemeteries is for a dog owned by the founder, Flora D'Auby Jenkins Kibbe. His name was Beau, and his epitaph reads, "No, Heaven will not / Ever Heaven be / Unless my dogs are there / To welcome me." Bideawee also claimed a milestone burial with a St. Bernard named Marshal Foch, named in honor of the French general who had served as supreme allied commander in World War I. The first high-profile case of an animal being rescued from medical experimentation, Marshal Foch was one of a group of dogs sent during the war to a laboratory at Bellevue Hospital to undergo a secret form of testing that was said to potentially benefit American soldiers overseas.

Exactly what was being done in the lab was never revealed, but at least four dogs were known to have been killed before Bideawee was able to intervene and rescue Marshal Foch. Although he arrived nervous and frightened, he intuitively understood what the organization's staff had done for him, and for the rest of his life was thankful and friendly towards them. He was appointed as the organization's official mascot, allowing him to socialize with the public, with whom he became a favorite. His recovery was a true success story. Sadly, however, he caught a cold after swimming in a lake at the association's country home in May 1924 and never fully recovered, dying the next month.

With New York State as the epicenter, pet cemeteries started to radiate out along the East Coast. Pine Ridge Pet Cemetery opened in Dedham, Massachusetts, in 1907 as the first to serve the Boston area. New Jersey had at least two by 1920, including one opened in Linwood in 1918 by Clara and Glen White, a married couple who were active in the local SPCA. It was a familiar story, the pair having no intention of getting into the pet cemetery business and merely looking for a place to bury their poodle. They chose a large lot that they owned behind their home, and then nailed a sign to a tree to let local pet owners know that they could likewise use the property. The response turned out to be far greater than they had imagined, at which point there was no turning back, and they dubbed the new cemetery Clara Glen, after their own first names.

Their cemetery would early on gain renown as the burial ground for pets from the nearby resort town of Atlantic City. Its greatest glory, however, did not come until 1952, and had nothing to do with high rollers on the boardwalk, but rather a simple mutt who was so beloved that his funeral turned into one of the most extraordinary ever recorded for an animal.[31] Nightlife lived up to his name. He may have been only a mongrel, but he lit up the scene anywhere he went—and he went wherever he wished. Owned by an Atlantic City bartender, he had free run of the city, stopping at restaurants and taverns to delight all he met, and hitching a ride with taxi drivers who knew where to drop him off when he wanted to return home.

Nightlife was felled on November 26 as he was crossing a road, victim of a motorist who waited too long before hitting the brakes. A local funeral parlor offered to host a wake for him, and as his body lay in a child's casket lined with white satin, his head tucked between his paws, an astonishing 2,000 people filtered through. All those who had known the spunky little dog had come to pay their respects, despite the fact that it was Thanksgiving Day and they would have to postpone their holiday plans to do so. The next day a procession headed out towards Clara Glen. Sixteen Cadillacs led the way, and more cars pulled into line behind them, stopping traffic for several blocks, with mourners on foot following by the hundreds. There was a racial aspect to all of this as well. It was a distinctly segregated area, and Nightlife's owner and most of his friends were black. Eventually, the police arrived on the scene. The police were white, yet they had not come to stop the procession but rather, with sirens flashing, to lead the little dog the rest of the way to his eternal home.

An entire city had effectively united in memory of a dog. When this throng arrived at

Both Frank Myers and Flora Kibbe founded pet cemeteries with the graves of their own dogs.

OVERLEAF: *Despite its unassuming graves, Friendship Grove holds a pedigree of over a century of service.*

CHUBBY CAT
1946
Loved By:
Dorothy Tingley

BEAUTY

KITTY
PAULINE MASON
DIED JULY 19 46 AGE 6 YRS.
OWNED

PEPPY
16 YEARS
BELOVED PET OF
MRS. DILLE, NEW YORK CITY

the graveside, floral arrangements were already in place around a bier, carrying such dedications as "To the most wonderful dog in the world." In his honor, a vocalist from one of the local nightclubs sang "My Buddy," an old standard from the 1920s, and a journalist read Vest's oration, but with the final lines changed to "Though Nightlife was of questionable origin, he truly was a pure-bred specimen of that noble line." Most remarkably of all, this outpouring of love had been arranged entirely by Nightlife's friends—the dog's owner, William Davis, was not even in town when he died.

Pennsylvania also had a smattering of pet cemeteries by the 1910s, including one in Radnor, about fifteen miles northwest of Philadelphia. It was part of the Francisvale Home for Small Animals, a facility founded in 1909 and named in honor of Francis, a stray dog taken in by the proprietor, Harriet Hare McClellan. She had discovered Francis huddled against the cold on a winter's night by the side of a road in Philadelphia in 1897. At the time, she was on her way to the opera, but she never arrived, having decided to tend the poor dog instead.

McClellan's love for him eventually became such that she started wondering how she could help the numerous other Francises on the city's streets. This was a time when, according to local law, a dog without a license could be shot on sight, so a shelter for homeless animals was dearly needed. McClellan founded Francisvale as a safe haven for those still living, with the attached cemetery honoring those among Philadelphia's pets who weren't. Francis then became one of the earliest burials, passing a year later, his headstone declaring him a "devoted friend and loving pet."

The nation's capital would certainly seem like prime real estate for a pet cemetery. There was, after all, a long-standing quote about the backstabbing and infighting there: "If you want a friend in Washington, get a dog."[32] Unfortunately, with strict regulations and steep fines governing the interment of animals on personal property, the District of Columbia

PREVIOUS: *Clara Glen deteriorated and its records are lost, but this is believed to be Nightlife's grave.*

Graves at Francisville for Francis and Jimmy MacCoy, whose epitaph became well known.

was no place to bury one. To solve that problem, a pet cemetery was in operation by 1902, adjacent to Mt. Olivet Cemetery and under the administration of a local veterinary office.

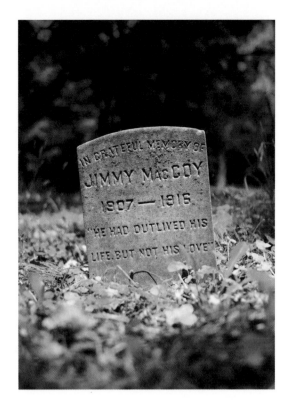

The cemetery failed, unfortunately, and little is known of its history. One curious grave inscription that was recorded, however, was for an English setter named Flash. The dog had attained considerable notoriety owing to his exceptional skill at stealing meat. Something of a bane to local butchers, he was said to have died at the age of fourteen after gorging himself on a sirloin steak pilfered from a stall on I Street. He was buried under a wooden marker bearing the legend, "Flash. He died leaving many friends, although probably not among the butchers."[33]

Residents of the capital had to wait until 1920 for another local option for their pets' final rites, when Aspin Hill Memorial Park opened, seven miles away in rural Maryland. Founded on eight acres by Richard and Bertha Birney, the cemetery was immediately popular, boasting 1,400 burials by the end of its first decade.[34] These included many for the animals owned by the nation's political elite, although the most remarked upon early gravestone speaks not to the halls of power, but rather to the heart of a mourning dog. Pal died in 1928, not long after his owner had drowned, the loss having plunged the pooch into a grief so desperate that he refused food and grew weaker and increasingly sickly. Kind-hearted people stepped in as potential owners, but the dog pined for the one he had lost. With his condition finally beyond hope, Pal was euthanized, passing on as a victim of despair. "He preferred death to life away from his master," reads his gravestone, which added a message to his former owner, in the hope that "This ever faithful barking ghost may leap to lick your phantom hand."[35]

Aspin Hill would grow into one of the most legendary American pet cemeteries, with more than 50,000 burials hosting a cadre of quirky characters. They range from Napoleon, a cat who could so correctly predict the weather by changing his sleeping position that farmers used to call his owner to find out the coming forecast, to the pets of J. Edgar Hoover, director of the FBI. Hoover distrusted people but greatly loved dogs, and there are rumors that he interred at least seven, although fittingly for a man whose career was in espionage, tracking them all down is no easy task. With a penchant for paranoid behavior, he was known to use pseudonyms when burying his animals, and he never came back to

visit them, or at least not publicly. Instead, he assigned one of the FBI's telephone operators the task of checking to make sure their graves were maintained.

Aspin Hill can also claim the smallest burial in any American pet cemetery: a grave for a fly. Its body arrived by mail in a jewel box, along with a note stating that it had lived in an office for a long time, and that, although the employees had at first found the fly annoying, they had eventually grown fond of it and hoped to give it a decent burial. A small grave was dug near a bush, but since no money had been included for a headstone, it went unmarked and the exact location is now unknown.

From the East Coast, pet cemeteries began expanding into the Midwest. A small burial ground had been opened in Wooster, Ohio, by 1906. It later vanished, but Brown Pet Cemetery, named after its founder, veterinarian Walter Brown, opened in 1924 in Columbus, and within a decade had become the largest outside of the East Coast states, with 1,000 graves.[36] Meanwhile, in Illinois, Hinsdale Animal Cemetery opened in 1926 in Clarendon Hills. The grounds initially spanned seven acres, and the front gate was inscribed,

IN FOND REMEMBRANCE OF OUR PET
1927 — SKIPPY — 1936

PREVIOUS: *The lamb—a symbol of innocence— marks the grave of Boysie, died 1946, at Clara Glen.*

Vintage photos from Aspin Hill: an admirer at the grave of Skippy and flowers offered to Napoleon.

"In life your truest pal, in death remember him." The cemetery was greatly needed since Chicago, only a few miles to the east, had grown to nearly 3 million residents. Plans for other local pet cemeteries in the 1910s had already fallen through, and a tragic turn of events only four years after Hinsdale opened—the original owner was killed in an automobile accident—could have added it to the list of those that fizzled out.

But the cemetery was purchased by John Stankowicz, a Russian émigré with a very good reason to want to honor deceased animals. During the communist takeover, Stankowicz had found himself a wanted man, slated for a firing squad. He did not hear the soldiers coming, but Arap, his shepherd–retriever mix, did. The dog began barking to sound the alarm, and Stankowicz, his wife, and his daughter all escaped through a back window, eventually making their way out of Russia and settling in Chicago in 1921. But Arap was not with them, having charged the soldiers to hold them off as his human family fled. As they did, they were forced to hear the gunshot that ended their faithful friend's life. It was an act of sacrifice one does not easily forget, and Stankowicz's first gesture as owner of the cemetery was to pay homage to the dog who had saved him. A life-sized iron statue was placed on a pedestal near the entrance, where it still stands. It bears Arap's name, and an inscription stating, "He gave up his life that a human might live. Greater love hath no man."

While the preceding represents only a very partial list of early American pet cemeteries, it must also include the first to be founded west of the Mississippi. The Oregon Humane Society in Portland opened its own burial ground in 1918, making it as old as some of the famous names on the East Coast. It was not until 1927, however, that it gained national recognition. "A great heart stopped this morning—the heart of Bobbie, the Silverton Wonder Dog," the newspapers declared on April 4, and an animal who had won the heart of the nation became the first famous burial on the West Coast.[37]

Part collie, part shepherd, Bobbie went missing in Wolcott, Indiana, in late 1923 while his family, the Braziers, were visiting relatives. Unable to find him, they eventually headed back to the West Coast, fearing the worst but hoping he would somehow make his way to the home of their local relations. Instead, Bobbie found his way back to Oregon. Over a six-month period, he undertook a grueling, 3,000-mile journey to seek out his family. He was near the point of collapse when he arrived in Silverton on February 15, 1924. But on seeing Nora, one of the family's children, in the street, Bobbie gathered

STRAY
1942 — 1958
LOVED PET OF

BABY
1959 — 1974
SWEETHEART
NEVER
FORGOTTEN
M. GERST

1953 - WHISKERS - 1967
OUR HEARTS BROKEN
WE'LL NEVER FORGET

DEAR KITTENS
MAR. 19 - MAY 23, 1972
P. & D. VONDERSMITH

his remaining strength for a sprint home, where he collapsed crying on the bed of his master, George Brazier.

Bobbie's incredible feat made him an icon to dog lovers worldwide. Yet despite his unmatched constitution, he was brought down by chewing on a bad bone, contracting ptomaine poisoning and dying at Rose City Animal Hospital at the age of six. The Humane Society provided his plot free of charge, and his coffin was a gift from the Great Northern Casket Company. Meanwhile, a local funeral home stepped in to take care of the other arrangements, and his doghouse was moved to the cemetery grounds and placed over his grave, behind a white picket fence. Originally, his tombstone could be seen through the windows, although it was later moved to the perimeter so the public could better view it.

Bobbie's doghouse grave was unconventional, but it received an impressive imprimatur four weeks later when Rin Tin Tin, Hollywood's biggest four-legged star, boarded a train for Portland. Although the ensuing event was a crass publicity stunt on the part of Warner Brothers Studios, as a dog in the 1920s, Bobbie could receive no higher honor than a visit from what amounted to canine royalty. As two hundred people gathered to cheer, Rin Tin Tin walked through the burial ground and laid a wreath at the grave. And as the story made the rounds, it underscored the point that, like Bobbie himself, pet cemeteries had completed their cross-country trek.

PREVIOUS: *Arap's statue at Hinsdale and photos from Oakleigh Pet Cemetery, an early Maryland burial ground.*   *Posthumous newspaper collage of Bobbie in front of his doghouse grave, present still in Portland.*

This is my humble prayer
Nor may I pray in vain
God make me good enough
To meet my Dog again

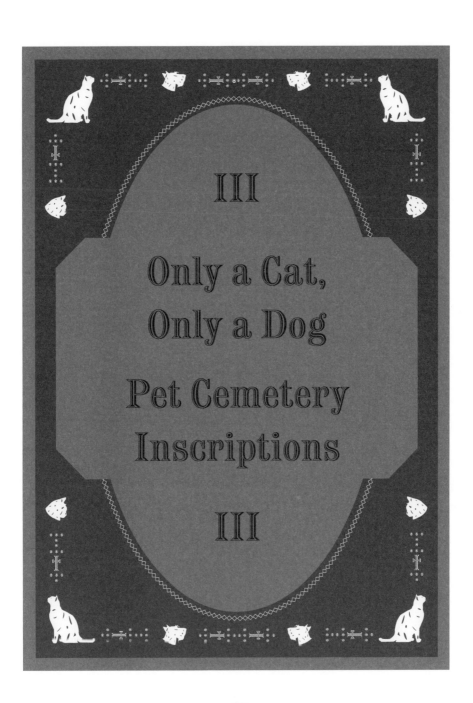

III

Only a Cat, Only a Dog

Pet Cemetery Inscriptions

III

Animal Gravestones:
Voices from the Past

Of all the surviving early American pet cemeteries, Pine Ridge in Dedham, Massachusetts, is the crown jewel. It has been operated since its inception by the Animal Rescue League of Boston, an organization founded by Anna Huntington Smith in 1899. She had spent her adult life in the service of animals after a neighbor casually mentioned that she intended to take her cat into the woods and leave it there when it became too old to catch mice. Horrified by such callousness, she vowed to create an organization for animal care, and had initially acquired the property in Dedham, ten miles southwest of the center of Boston, as a place to send malnourished and abused horses in the hope they could be made well by the peace and harmony of the New England countryside.

The cemetery was established on a corner of this land in 1907 to provide residents of the Boston Bay a place to inter their pets. Pine Ridge never quite matched the stature of its rivals, however. It cannot claim the pedigree of Hartsdale, for example, and it certainly does not compare to the massive size of Aspin Hill. Nonetheless, it has something uniquely its own, something so precious that it makes visiting an unrivaled experience: it is a time capsule. While the rest of America's early pet cemeteries changed drastically as newer graves were placed in the same ground as the older ones, which often became obscured or were sometimes even removed, Pine Ridge took a different approach. When its initial plot was deemed sufficiently full, new burials were moved to a completely different part of the property, thus preserving the original grounds. The appearance of the older cemetery is not entirely unscathed. Certain glorious touches, such as a 200-foot grape arbor that once lined its pathway, have been lost. But the grounds remain intact enough from modern intrusion that visiting can feel like entering a fairytale.

As a paved walkway leads west past the campus's main offices and kennels, cresting a small hill, a field containing hundreds of magnificent little graves comes into view below, a whimsical sight lovingly maintained in a large clearing bordered by thick groves of barberry bushes and cedar trees. The sounds of the street are muffled as the visitor descends the path, replaced instead by the chirps of birds and the rustling of squirrels. If one visits on a spring day, small dots of bright color pepper the lush greens, as flowers wake from their winter's sleep. The modern world fades away, and it feels as if one has traveled back in time to the 1930s, when one could take a train from Boston's South Station to the Dedham terminal, and from there pay a 25-cent carriage fee to continue on to this arcadian animal necropolis.

In those days, some of the animals buried at Pine Ridge were famous. There is Igloo, for instance, the world's most traveled fox terrier, a favorite of the press for having accompanied his human companion, Admiral Richard Byrd, on expeditions to both the North and South Poles. Igloo wore a canvas suit sewn by a sail maker to protect him from the cold, and his hobbies included chasing emperor penguins—until one taught him better by slapping him in the face with a wing. He died in 1931 and his unique gravestone is appropriately shaped like the tip of an iceberg.

Another famous—or perhaps we should say infamous—burial is for three Boston terriers owned by the accused axe murderess Lizzie Borden. Despite an acquittal, the stigma of being the defendant in the most publicized trial of the era hounded Lizzie for the rest of her life, and even followed her dogs to their grave. Named Donald Stuart, Laddie Nelson, and Royal Miller, they were interred together in a single plot pushed to a corner of the cemetery, at the very edge of the impenetrable brush, so that no one else's pets would have to be buried too near those owned by a woman of dubious reputation.

Impossible to miss along the path is one of the most ostentatious graves ever commissioned for an animal: a stone tomb with a large bronze door that looks like something from *Lord of the Rings*. It is in memory of Jessie, a dog owned by Boston merchant R. H. White. While it trumps all the others in terms of

OVERLEAF: *Igloo's funeral and visitors to his grave, plus Jessie's monumental mausoleum door.*

grandiosity, the exquisite carving found among the more humble graves means there are numerous miniature masterpieces to be found. There is a small, delicately rendered bust of a French bulldog, for example, that seems to emerge watchfully out of the grass. Almost next to it is a beautifully sculpted stone cat resting upon a dais marking the burial spot of Frisky and Paul Nemo, the feline friends of the Boston socialite Mrs. D. M. Clapp. And nearby is the delightful touch of a grave marker carved as a satchel from which a small dog enthusiastically emerges—there is no name attached to it, but we can easily imagine it as a scene from life, when the little pooch would travel with its owner.

The true treasures here, however, are the words these graves bear. Pine Ridge is the world's greatest trove of older pet cemetery inscriptions preserved in one place without modern intrusion, and like voices from the past whispering in the breeze, they still have much to tell us. Inscriptions on pets' grave markers speak in their own peculiar idiom, free from the restraints that govern our discourse over the human dead. People tend to comment freely about their animals, and the emotion can be raw and direct, alternately heartbreaking, heartwarming, hilarious, tragic, or all of these at the same time.

Gravestones for pets can say almost anything, and that randomness is part of their beauty. Their words can be lyrical in their simplicity, such as "Fudge, as dear and sweet as his name," at Exbury Gardens in Southampton, England. Other times they are crass, as with a grave marker in a desert pet cemetery in Ajo, Arizona. There was apparently some kind of family squabble about a dog named Ringo, and the inscription makes no bones about where the owner's loyalty fell: "Best dog. Everyone loved you except Uncle Ted. Yeah, fuck Uncle Ted."

However pets' inscriptions are worded, certain themes have long been common. The most dominant is friendship, and all told there may be thousands of grave markers in pet cemeteries that declare an animal to have been a person's best friend, or even their only friend. Statements of love, thanks,

PREVIOUS: *The delicately sculpted cat that serves as a grave marker for Frisky and Paul Nemo.*

The epitaph for Fudge is found on one of three dog graves at Exbury Gardens in Southampton.

or the depth of loss are also obvious choices. Various literary inspirations might be quoted to express these sentiments, or at least echo in original epitaphs they have influenced. Prominent among them is a pet-loss poem known as "They Will Not Go Quietly." Its seventeen lines remind the reader of the continued feeling of a pet's loving presence, that "In subtle ways they let us know / their spirit still survives," and how "That one place in our heart / belongs to them / and always will."[1]

Another mourning text, which was not specifically written for animals but has nonetheless greatly influenced animal epitaphs, is a poem popularly titled "Don't Weep for Me." Its haunting single stanza urges the mourner to understand all the ways the deceased lives on. "I am the thousand winds that blow," it promises, as well as "the sunlight on ripened grain" and the "soft star that shines at night." There is no need to weep at the grave, the poem promises, because "I am not there, I did not die."[2]

The most influential literary inspiration, however, is a paragraph-long prose poem written by a Scottish teenager in 1959. On the death of her dog Major, Edna Clyne pulled a sheet of paper from her sister's notebook and began writing about a bridge leading to an Elysian field where the souls of pets would await their human companions, so that together they could cross over into eternity, never again to be parted.[3] Under the title "Rainbow Bridge," her text went on to become ubiquitous in pet mourning circles.

Not only are references to the "Rainbow Bridge" commonly found in epitaphs, the entirety is sometimes reproduced on huge stone tablets on pet cemetery grounds, giving it an authority that could rival anything Moses carried down from Mount Sinai. What young Edna had accomplished was to create a specific vision of another theme that had long been common in animal epitaphs: the desire for reunion. References are found as far back as Hyde Park and Molesworth, while one of the early gravestones at the Cimetière des Chiens went so far as to declare that the owner would forgo Heaven if a dog named Sapho were not also allowed entry. "If thy soul, Sapho, cannot go on with mine, / Oh dear and noble friend, through all of life to be, / Then I desire no Heaven, may my fate be like thine, / Here to come at last, to dreamless sleep with thee."[4]

Apparent family squabbles didn't prevent Ringo from being laid to rest with love in the Arizona desert.

OVERLEAF: *A version of the "Rainbow Bridge" text as it appears at the Los Angeles Pet Memorial Park.*

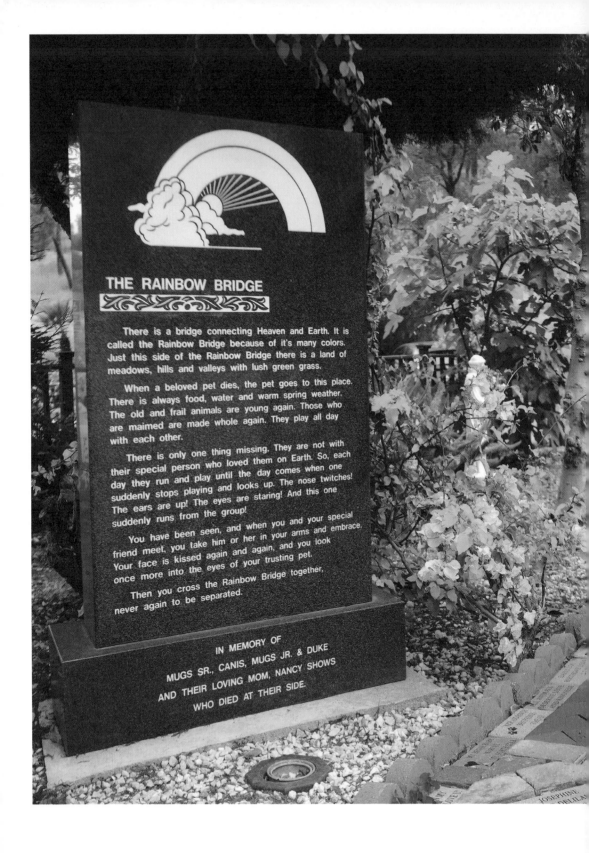

THE RAINBOW BRIDGE

There is a bridge connecting Heaven and Earth. It is called the Rainbow Bridge because of it's many colors. Just this side of the Rainbow Bridge there is a land of meadows, hills and valleys with lush green grass.

When a beloved pet dies, the pet goes to this place. There is always food, water and warm spring weather. The old and frail animals are young again. Those who are maimed are made whole again. They play all day with each other.

There is only one thing missing. They are not with their special person who loved them on Earth. So, each day they run and play until the day comes when one suddenly stops playing and looks up. The nose twitches! The ears are up! The eyes are staring! And this one suddenly runs from the group!

You have been seen, and when you and your special friend meet, you take him or her in your arms and embrace. Your face is kissed again and again, and you look once more into the eyes of your trusting pet.

Then you cross the Rainbow Bridge together, never again to be separated.

IN MEMORY OF
MUGS SR., CANIS, MUGS JR. & DUKE
AND THEIR LOVING MOM, NANCY SHOWS
WHO DIED AT THEIR SIDE.

DON'T WEEP FOR ME

DO NOT STAND AT MY GRAVE AND WEEP;
I AM NOT THERE.
I DO NOT SLEEP.
I AM A THOUSAND WINDS THAT BLOW;
I AM THE DIAMOND GLINTS ON SNOW;
I AM THE SUNLIGHT ON RIPENED GRAIN;
I AM THE GENTLE AUTUMN RAIN.
WHEN YOU AWAKEN IN THE MORNING'S HUSH,
I AM THE SWIFT UPLIFTING RUSH OF QUIET
BIRDS IN CIRCLED FLIGHT;
I AM THE SOFT STAR THAT SHINES AT NIGHT.
DO NOT STAND BY MY GRAVE AND CRY;
I AM NOT THERE;
I DID NOT DIE.

ANON

Epitaphs for pets also frequently extol an animal's virtues, enumerating such qualities as faith, honesty, and integrity. While we consider these traits a moral foundation that sets human beings apart from animals, we often see in pets a more perfected version of our own ideal. As an example, the centerpiece monument at Clara Glen Pet Cemetery, dedicated to the dogs owned by its founders, declares that "The loyalty of a dog may well put most men to shame, for few are as loyal to their heavenly master as the humble dog is to his earthly one." That an animal's virtues paradoxically make them seem at least as "human" as we is noted on one of the early surviving gravestones at Hartsdale. We are told that Sydney, who died in 1902, was "born a dog / [but] lived like a gentleman."

Gravestone inscriptions are not static, however. They have evolved according to patterns that reveal much about the relationship between humans and animals at a given time and place. On the whole, early grave markers tended to say very little. They often gave only an animal's name, although in many cases they did not even give that, frequently offering the owner's identity instead, or listing the deceased simply as "Pet." If they did say more, it was often with a lack of emotion. This can seem cold nowadays, but the restraint was typical of the time, influenced by the desire of pet owners to not appear overly sentimental.

For similar reasons, through the first two decades of the 20th century, pets were more likely to be referred to as a "friend" than as a family member. Nevertheless, there were a few brave souls who used familial terms, such as on a gravestone at Molesworth, dated Easter Sunday, 1905, dedicated to Chun and inscribed, "With his mother's fondest love / Ever in dearest remembrance / Of her sweet little companion." This was a trend that did not fundamentally change until the 1920s and 1930s, when ambiguous terms that obliquely imply a more intimate relationship became popular. Calling a pet a "baby," for instance, became more common, or according to another grave from Hartsdale, "He was one of us." Proclaiming familial relations remained rare until the second half of the 20th century, although by now it is typical to find a pet referred to as a son or daughter, or the owner as the animal's parent.

Another quirk of older animal graves is that when a more expansive epitaph was offered, it was not unusual to mention how the animal died, and often in stark terms. This was common in Hyde Park. Monty, for example, was "Drowned in Old Windsor Lock." He was at least given a "Gone but not forgotten," to round out his epitaph, but Scamp was "Run over" and there was nothing more to be said. We might call these "cause of death" gravestones, and the plethora of examples at other cemeteries include "Run over by a tractor," "Death by wasp," and, simply, "Lung abscess." To a modern viewer, such inscriptions can appear

PREVIOUS: *"Don't Weep for Me," the original dated to 1935, set in stone at Angel's Rest in Utah.*

An epitaph for Bingo at Pet Heaven, founded in 1942 as the first pet cemetery in Atlanta.

BEROL'S
BESSIE IOLA
FEB. 1, 1953 · JUNE 6, 1957
A WONDERFUL
BITCH WITH A SAD
ENDING

IN MEMORY OF
A LOVING PET
"JUDY"
KILLED BY A TRACTOR.
1957 - 1967.
"SHE NEVER TOLD A LIE."

DICKINSO

callous, although some at least added a moral twist. A headstone from Friendship Grove in Hornell, for instance, was addressed to the person who poisoned a local dog. It includes the remonstrance that the dog that died "did his part as a companion with a kinder heart" than "a dog like you."

Early graves also tended to avoid religious symbolism, even without a mandate like the one issued at the Cimetière des Chiens. Animals, of course, tend to be mum on their own spiritual leanings, so even as it has become more acceptable, there remains a question as to whether the use of sacred iconography on a pet's gravestone is appropriate. A popular middle ground has long been to note the angelic qualities of a pet, commend them to God's care, or use quotes from sacred texts as an epitaph.

An example of this approach, also at Hartsdale, is found on a grave dated 1941, the inscription reading, "Rags, thou knowest that I love thee," with a specific reference to John 21:17. This is the biblical passage in which Peter professes for the third time his love for Christ, lest it be doubted. In the context of Rags's grave, the owner apparently wished it to be known that the affection felt for the pet was equally unshakeable. Biblical quotes that stress an animal's innocence, such as Matthew 5:8 from Christ's Sermon on the Mount, have also been popular. "Blessed are the pure in heart, for they will see God," for instance, is prominently displayed on a headstone at Aspin Hill.

On the other side of the coin, there has never been a problem with giving the Devil his due. Diabolic names have always been common for pets, especially

A curious epitaph at a cemetery for bird dogs founded in Georgia by pencil magnate Henry Berol.

Grave at the Rossendale pet cemetery in England for a dog killed in an apparent farming accident.

for black cats or dogs as nods to various stories from mythology and folklore that associated these animals with occult powers. Such names became especially popular in the 1960s and 1970s, no doubt spurred by the growing prominence of the occult in popular culture, and it is hard nowadays to find a pet cemetery that does not have at least a couple of Satans or Lucifers.

The occult content generally stops at the name, although in some cases owners or visitors have been inspired to leave little statues or offerings at graves of pets named after the Devil, especially around Halloween. In one instance, at Sea Breeze Pet Cemetery in Huntington Beach, California, the occult theme is carried over into a cryptic inscription underneath the name Satan, where the capital letters "T B D C T E L" appear. At first glance, the viewer might wonder whether this is an attempt at some kind of curse. Not in the least. In fact, it is a pun on behalf of the owner: what initially comes across as occult is instead an acronym for "The Best Damned Cat to Ever Live."

Strolling the grounds of early pet cemeteries in particular can provide some curious encounters for a modern visitor, since many once common names and phrases now seem inappropriate. Modern cat owners are far more

The devil gets his due at this black cat's grave, decorated for Halloween at a California cemetery.

OVERLEAF: *The term "dumb" means "mute" on this memorial to Trixie in Ilford, England.*

In memory of our dumb frie[nd]
the dog that GOD gave u[s]
"TRIXIE"
BORN 26th FEBRUARY 19[..]
F[E]LL ASLEEP 31st OCTOBER 19[..]

judicious about feline nicknames that are too easily associated with female genitalia, for instance. The "Beloved Pussy" buried in Happy Woodlawn in 1941, or the "Seven Wonder Pussies" interred in Aspin Hill, were no doubt all fine cats, but their epitaphs now sound more like something from a bordello than a pet cemetery. It is also unlikely that people will eulogize a female dog as a "bitch" any time soon, although this too had once been common. A bird dog cemetery in Waynesboro, Georgia, has one such inscription that is sure to stop any modern visitor: "A wonderful bitch with a sad ending."

Other words that can cause confusion include "smut." Nowadays, the word is associated with lascivious material, but it had once been a popular pet name due to a prior meaning, when it had been synonymous with soot. We can therefore safely rest assured that pets named Smut were not involved in pornography, but simply had dark colored coats. Old graves also frequently make references to animals being dumb. One of the grandest burials at the pet cemetery run by the People's Dispensary for Sick Animals in Ilford, east London, is dedicated to a dog named Trixie and

bears the inscription, "In memory of our dumb friend / the dog that God gave us." Trixie's owners were not publicly lamenting God having offered them an idiot, however. "Dumb" had been a common synonym for mute and was frequently used by early activists to express the idea that animals were voiceless and in need of human champions to speak out on their behalf. The first journal in the United States dedicated to animal welfare, established in 1868 and published by the Massachusetts SPCA, was even titled *Our Dumb Animals*.

While many names and terms faded into the past, they were replaced by those pulled from popular culture. During the second half of the 20th century, people increasingly began naming their pets after movie, literary, or pop culture characters. This eventually became one of the largest categories of pet names, and it is now possible to stroll a pet cemetery grounds and meet anyone from Sir Lancelot to Dracula, and in between find Yoda, Lady Macbeth, the entire cast of characters from Marvel comics, and pretty much anyone else you can imagine, fictive or not, who has attained even a moderate level of fame.

Yoda's grave is found in California, not Degobah, plus a sentiment felt by countless mourning pet owners.

OVERLEAF: *A beloved pussy laid to rest in Canada's first pet cemetery, Happy Woodland, near Toronto.*

While having a general guide to the evolution of grave markers for pets provides us with useful insights, it is also best to not be overly analytical. The exceptions are almost as common as the rules, since the guiding principle behind them has always been the human heart. Better in that case to return to Pine Ridge and listen to the voices of the past. "He was more than a friend," Admiral Byrd offered about Igloo, a deliberate understatement to be sure, since that is the least he might say when discussing a dog who accompanied him to the very ends of the Earth. "Sleeping awhile" graces the grave of Lizzie Borden's dogs. Beautiful in its brevity, the epitaph manages with two words to deflect death, a topic that had defined Lizzie's life.

Others offer poetry. A dog named Prince who died in 1926, "My devoted companion," is commended to the Almighty with verses taken from Alfred, Lord Tennyson, reminding us of the value of all living things to their Creator: "That nothing walks with aimless feet / That not one life shall be destroyed / Or cast as rubbish to the void / When God hath made the pile complete." Meanwhile, a grave marked with the name Kruger quotes the Scottish poet Thomas Campbell: "To live in the hearts we leave behind is not to die." Le Baron Cooke, a Boston poet, would compose his own words for the grave of Pierrot, and while they are far more simple, he could not have expressed the sentiment better if he had written a book: "I knew love; I had a dog."

Delightful names are of course found throughout. "Hardy Tarfoot, A faithful little friend," rests by the curve of the hill. Nearby is a bird dog with the officious-sounding name of Rover Birderius, while a short walk leads to Toddle the Troll—breed unknown, actual troll unlikely. Yet as charming as this all is, none of these animals are the cemetery's headline attraction. He rests in a small grave in the southwest corner of the grounds. An unlikely star, he is famous now in death despite there having been no record preserved of him in life. And it is all thanks to the voice that still speaks from his gravestone, simple words offered at his passing, but rendered so exquisitely that they have trumped all the others. And not just at Pine Ridge, because his has become the world's best-known pet cemetery inscription, and there is no close second.

More Than a Pet?
More Than a Phrase

The headstone stands about a foot and a half high, tapering towards the top and culminating in a scroll on each side, between which the name Dewey stands in relief, in thick letters above the dates 1898–1910. As the stone has exfoliated over time and fallen further behind in its continued battle against moss, the

words inscribed on its face have become harder to read. It helps if the sun is at an oblique angle to cast shadows into the delicate incisions, but they are still legible, even if one must squint to see them. In five short lines, they read, "'He was only a cat' but he was human enough to be a great comfort in hours of loneliness and pain."

There is perfection to the words. Dewey is not the only comforter buried at Pine Ridge—a mere stone's throw away is a grave for Midget, likewise from 1910, inscribed, "She shared my joy and wiped away my tears." And Dewey is certainly not the only feline among the early burials. Also nearby is a grave, perhaps even older, dedicated to "A noble cat." Yet no one stops for these graves, no one shares their images. It is Dewey's that resonates. Humble wording cannot hide the epitaph's hubris, it is clear that whoever commissioned the stone considered Dewey to be considerably more than "only a cat." The sentiment strikes an emotional chord with anyone who has ever taken solace in an animal. Who among us has not known one like him, an animal companion that is something far greater, one with the power to work magic on the human heart? The memory of such beloved pets is immediately summoned for the viewer, and feline aficionados have shared photos of the headstone incessantly on social media, resulting in many millions of views, along with torrents of "oohs," "awws," and all manner of broken-heart emojis.

The most commonly seen image of the grave, shot in 2018, was named by a pet-themed website as the most iconic animal photo in history, while publications covering social media have based entire stories around it.[5] Predictably, the same photo has also been used as clickbait by marketers who are not above tugging on heartstrings in order to steer eyes to their accounts. But the modern response to Dewey's grave is not new. It has been singled out as special for over a century. Within a decade of the cat's passing it was already being celebrated, by a journalist from the *Boston Globe* who in 1920 praised the inscription as "full of human suffering and feline devotion."[6]

A year later, the *Boston Post* declared the gravestone to be "worthy of a place in feline history."[7] This was prescient as it turned out, and not only because Dewey's cultish following has grown with time. His grave marker indeed owns a special place in history, as the oldest surviving memorial in a pet cemetery that makes a public statement about the role a cat played in the life of its human companion. Those for previous cats, which were no doubt beloved pets, tend to be ambiguous, like the "noble cat" nearby. But Dewey's epitaph is an unequivocal statement of love and gratitude. Such declarations had been previously reserved for dogs, making Dewey's gravestone the great ancestor of the countless heartfelt memorials to cats that would come afterward.

Dewey's epitaph is shrouded in mystery, but has nevertheless become a favorite among cat lovers.

Despite its historical importance, no one seems to know anything about the grave beyond the inscription itself. When photos of it are shared, they are usually devoid of any explanation or context, as if the grave exists detached from history. This is hardly the fault of the people doing the sharing, however, since no background has ever been put forward. No primary sources exist pertaining to either the cat's life or death, and the newspaper articles from the 1920s that extoled the epitaph told nothing of the story behind it, as if it had already faded from memory. This has left Dewey as a cat more mythic than real, and the identity of his owner and the grief this person suffered a mystery.

With clues to the story behind the world's most famous cat grave scarce, we must turn for meaning to the inscription itself. Its three key words, "only a cat," reveal more than we might initially guess. In merely eight letters, they invite us down a long and circuitous path with stops at burials both loving and infamous. While the phrase is now forgotten, it was once famous across the United States, even inspiring an entire genre of poems and short stories. These three words take us into the very heart of pet ownership in the late 19th and early 20th centuries, so if we hope to meet Dewey, we must start by learning what it meant to be "only a cat."

Not only was the phrase not invented by Dewey's owner, by the time of his death it had been in circulation for more than three decades. As on the gravestone, the phrase was almost always set in quotation marks. This was intended as a hint to the reader that it should not be taken literally. Rather, it served as a form of mockery towards people who could not understand the relationship one might have with a companion feline: it might be "only a cat" to the unenlightened, but those who had loved such animals knew their true value.

But the meaning ran deeper still, as an editorialist named Eva DeMarsh explained in a 1918 issue of *Our Dumb Animals*.[8] The phrase was born in the face of an overwhelmingly negative attitude towards felines. This was a time when most people knew cats solely as strays that scavenged in the streets, and whose caterwauling in alleys kept them up at night. Back then, they were stereotyped

THE DEAD OF NIGHT.

Cruelty to cats was so acceptable that it served as the subject of this 1901 tobacco card.

as unaffectionate, disloyal, capricious, and far inferior to dogs. The popular judgment was that cats were little more than a public nuisance and could be freely subjected to inhumane treatment.

Recounting for her readers the calumnies and abuses cats were commonly subjected to, DeMarsh revealed that "'Only a cat'" is in truth "a synonym of many a cruelty." More than a phrase, it was an attitude that held cats to be of no consequence. "Why throw sticks and stones at them," she asked, "or begrudge them a bite from the garbage can?" The question was of course rhetorical, with the answer being that it was "'Only a cat!'" But "within every one lies the power of suffering," she continued, turning the phrase on its head by recounting a cat's many virtues and focusing on their capacity to care about their human companions. Even if one is "'Only a cat,'" she concluded, "in that little body dwells a heart capable of such love and devotion as would put you and me to shame." "Only a cat" thereby became a rehabilitated phrase, transformed by feline fanciers from an insult into a rallying cry.

There is a curious twist to the phrase's history, however. Despite its importance to cat lovers, they themselves did not invent it. They had instead appropriated it from dog lovers, for whom "only a dog" had become a well-established stock phrase during the 1870s, likewise inspiring poems, short stories, and gravestone inscriptions. Its genesis can be credited to a New Yorker named Francis Butler. A veterinarian by trade, Dr. Butler's love for canines ultimately cost him his life—he died in 1874 after contracting rabies—but not before he had authored various training manuals and breed guides. The literary output that survives him in addition includes numerous memorials and epitaphs. In remembrance of a setter named Shot, for instance, he penned these lines:

> Good stranger pause! nor dare to laugh,
> To read a canine Epitaph!
>
> No sculpted urn, nor chiselled marble fair,
> Recalls to light, imperfect manhood here;
> Here rests a name, which ne'er should be forgot:
> The staunch and faithful perfect setter, Shot,
> No crime to expiate, no soul to save;
> No demon haunts the slumber of his grave,
> *Hic Jacet* Shot, an honest, well trained setter,
> And lucky who e'ver may own a better.[9]

He also wrote a series of verses on the passing of his Siberian bloodhound Moscow in 1862. These were apparently written at the dog's graveside—she was, he told his readers, "Just six feet hence, beneath the chilly ground"—and declared her to have been:

MASSIVE IN LIMB, YET LIGHT, SYMMETRIC, GAY;
TRUSTY COMPANION OF MY LONELY WAY—
BY DAY SO GENTLE, SOCIABLE, AND MILD;
BY NIGHT A TIGRESS; WATCHFUL, FIERCE AND WILD.[10]

Any judgment of Butler's memorials is of course subjective, although in assessing the general consensus it suffices to say that they have never found a place among the great odes to dogs. But within his body of work, the fifth and seventh lines of an epitaph for a King Charles spaniel stood out, containing three words that lived on long after their author's death:

LEGAL DESCENDANT OF A SIRE,
ONE PASSING TEAR I CRAVE;
ONE TENDER TRIBUTE ONLY I DESIRE,
TREAD SOFTLY ON MY GRAVE—
ONLY A DOG! 'TIS TRUE, YET WHERE'S THE MAN,
WHO NE'ER BETRAYED HIS TRUST?
ONLY A DOG! WHAT BIPED DARE OR CAN

*One of this boy's dogs was hit by a car. The driver
yelled, "It's only a dog!"*

REVILE MY SLEEPING DUST?
MY WASTED FORM LIES CHILL BENEATH THE GROUND
BUT HERE MY TROUBLES CEASE;
LET TERROR STRIKE WHEN THE LAST TRUMP SHALL SOUND
I'LL STILL SLEEP ON IN PEACE.[11]

"Only a dog!," presented as a challenge and repeated for impact, resonated with dog lovers. The rest of the poem was soon forgotten, but "only a dog" began to appear in epitaphs and eulogies by other writers. In 1876, a Vermont newspaper used the phrase as the title of an unattributed memorial presented in the form of a short story that told of a six-year-old dog whose owners had recently died.[12] The dog was sent to live with their relatives, and while they loved him and he returned their affections, he nonetheless fell victim to inexorable sadness over the loss of his previous human companions. Possessed of a broken heart that could not be mended, he became weaker by the day until he himself died a few months later. "'Only a dog,'" the new owners commented in their emotional conclusion, the phrase now placed in quotation marks to acknowledge his worth was far greater, "yet we weep for him!"

Over the next two decades, verses based around the words "only a dog" coalesced into their own category of literature in the United States. The phrase especially appealed to amateur poets who, like Dr. Butler, possessed a sentimentality that might be hackneyed, but whose love for canines was beyond reproach. Among them was a woman named Nettie E. Nicol, who composed one of the most influential works in the genre. Its verses feature "Only a dog" at the beginning of each stanza, and the final set of rhymes, in which she dreams of a possible reunion after she herself has passed, sounds something like a precursor to the "Rainbow Bridge."

"ONLY A DOG," YOU SAY, AND SNEER,
AS I WIPE AWAY A GATHERING TEAR.
ONLY A DOG, WITH A NATURE GRAND.
SOMEHOW HE ALWAYS WOULD UNDERSTAND.
TO ME, HE WAS EVER LOVING AND KIND;
FRIENDS SO TRUE ARE MOST HARD TO FIND.

ONLY A DOG; BUT I LOVED HIM WELL;
LOVED HIM BETTER THAN WORDS CAN TELL.
YOU SHRUG YOUR SHOULDERS AND TURN AWAY,
"WELL, I WOULDN'T SHED TEARS FOR A DOG," YOU SAY.
AND YET MY FRIEND YOU WOULD WISH TO BE!
GOD KEEP SUCH FRIENDSHIP FAR FROM ME!

Only a dog; but his soft brown eyes
Looked into mine so loving and wise;
Eager to follow where'er I might roam
Wherever I wandered to him it was home.
Contented and happy, always the same,
To rest in the shadow or romp in the game.

Only a dog! But his heart was true
Whether the skies were gray or blue;
Always faithful, whate'er might betide,
Content to linger by my side.
Whether I gave him a smile or a frown
Love looked out from his eyes so brown.

Only a dog; lying so still;
Whistle or call him, do what I will.
He never can come, or hear me again;
Though I watch and wait it is all in vain.
My playmate and friend, I grieve for you
Of all my companions most tried and true.

Only a dog, but the love he gave
Cannot have perished in the grave;

So constant and faithful and true in heart
Must in eternity have some part.
And I sometimes think, when I've crossed life's sea
I'll find him waiting to welcome me.[13]

The Nicol poem was written sometime in the final decades of the 19th century, and its popularity with readers was such that it continued to be reprinted through the 1930s. But of all the "only a dog" poems, the one that gained the greatest notoriety is titled "Flight." The phrase "only a dog" appears twice, both times in the third of its three stanzas, and it became popular in syndication after appearing as a canine obituary in the *New York Evening Post*.[14]

Never again shall her leaping welcome
Greet me when coming at eventide;
Never again shall her glancing footfall
Range the fallow from side to side.
Under the raindrops, under the snowflakes,
Down in a narrow and darksome bed,
Safe from sorrow or fear or loving,
Lieth my beautiful, still and dead.

Mouth of silver, and skin of satin,
Foot as fleet as an arrow's flight,
Statue-still at the call of "steady,"
Eyes as clear as the stars of night.
Laughing breadths of yellow stubble
Now shall rustle to alien tread,
And rabbits run in the dew-dim clover
Safe—for my beautiful lieth dead.

Only a dog, do you say, Sir Critic?
Only a dog, but as truth I prize,
The truest love I have won in living
Lived in the deeps of her limpid eyes.
Frosts of winter nor heat of summer
Could make her fail if my footsteps led,
And memory holds in its treasure casket,
The name of my darling who lieth dead.

*Surviving family at the funeral of a poodle named
Buster Snook at Aspin Hill in 1921.*

"Flight" was a cut above its kindred works, rising from the newspaper syndication circuit to be included in poetry reviews. The author was a Miss M. A. Collins of Tennessee, although she never got the credit she deserved since the *Evening Post* had attributed the poem to "S.M.A.C.," and it continued to appear only under those mysterious initials.[15] Magazines dedicated to dog afficionados even published pleas that someone identify the author, but to no avail.[16] Perhaps the reason the author herself never came forward was that her work proved so popular as to become notorious for its connection to one of the biggest scandals of the 1880s involving a pet's burial.

This unlikely turn of events came about thanks to Rose Halladay Howe, a wealthy New Yorker and the widow of Elias Howe, Jr., an inventor who patented the lockstitch for sewing machines. The death of Rose's pug Fannie at the age of twelve on December 10, 1881, was a devastating loss, and she put her considerable wealth to work commemorating the dog. Fannie, "well known throughout canine good society" according to the *Brooklyn Daily Eagle*, was memorialized in an opulent service in which she was seen lying in state, wrapped in gold cloth and encased in a glass-topped silver casket surrounded by a mountain of flowers.[17] The program included a minister reciting an oration and a vocal quartet singing Stephen Foster's "Old Dog Tray," the lyrics of which tell of a man at the end of his life who comes to realize that the greatest and most loyal friend he has ever had was his canine companion.

While all of this was considered eccentric, none of it was cause for a scandal. But Rose pushed things too far. The Howes owned a family plot at Green-Wood Cemetery in Brooklyn, and in a highly visible location. A large Quincy granite headstone suddenly appeared there, inscribed with the final eight lines of "Flight," starting with the first "Only a dog," and Rose announced that it was at that spot, in a cemetery intended for humans, that Fannie had been buried. We've seen enough examples to know how this will end up, and in the case of Green-Wood the cemetery was especially sensitive due to an incident only two years prior.

In 1879, Lemuel Wilmarth, a painter and one of the founders of the Art Students League of New York, provided a lavish funeral at his family plot for a Newfoundland named Gipsy. This was justified, Wilmarth asserted, by the dog's accomplishments in life. The list, which may or may not be credible, included having rescued Mrs. Wilmarth from drowning and living to the age of twenty-three—seemingly impossible since the breed typically lives eight to ten years. Whatever the truth of Wilmarth's claims, he clearly loved the dog, and to demonstrate the depth of his affections he had Gipsy delivered to the graveside

Despite being the subject of controversy, Fannie's gravestone remains in the Howe family plot.

in a custom casket carried on a large silver plate escorted by two carriages. He then had a marker listing her virtues placed over the burial site. Newspapers along the East Coast wrote up the proceedings, and the cemetery received a flurry of complaints from angry clients who did not want their relatives' graves in the same ground as a dog.[18]

Gipsy's grave marker was quickly removed, although curiously there is no record of the dog herself being exhumed. It is in fact suspected she is still present, and the burial spot was re-memorialized in 2007, marked by a plaque inscribed with a poem by Henry Bergh, founder of the ASPCA, who had found inspiration in Wilmarth's love for his dog. Whatever the case—whether Gipsy had in fact been exhumed or Green-Wood's administration had simply removed the visual evidence—Rose Halladay Howe was on dangerous ground, especially considering that in the wake of the Wilmarth episode the cemetery's administration had officially forbidden any further burial of pets. As a courtesy, it ruled that the stone itself could stay on the Howe plot, and it remains there to this day. But Fannie would have to go.

We can only speculate as to what happened next because Rose and the cemetery offered different versions of the story. According to Rose, Fannie remained interred at the location marked by the headstone. She insisted on this until her own death in 1890, when she was buried just a few steps away. Her friends afterward continued to claim that the pug was there, at her mistress's side. The cemetery, on the other hand, was equally insistent that the prohibition on the burial of dogs at Green-Wood had been enforced and that Fannie was not buried on the property. As far as they were aware, Fannie had been re-interred in Rose's own backyard. Obviously, one side was lying, and unless the plot is someday exhumed we may never know which. However that may be, the affair garnered enough publicity to introduce the term "only a dog" to a far wider public. And among those who took notice were cat lovers.

 ### *The Search for Dewey:*
Context, History . . . and an Identity?

If dog owners thought they had a hard time making outsiders understand their affections, they knew nothing of the plight faced by the feline faction. Dogs were at least respectable animals in the 19th century, but simply owning a cat, an animal still not completely rehabilitated from a long-standing association with heresy and witchcraft, was in and of itself considered borderline eccentric. For those who loved an animal so misunderstood, the phrase "only a cat" would take on added importance, and Dewey's is hardly the only gravestone to have

carried the words. "Only a cat" is found in various other pet cemeteries, and over a wide range of dates. It serves as the sole epitaph for Minnie on a grave from the 1930s at Aspin Hill, for example. And the phrase had enough longevity to be current even into the 1960s, a grave marker found at an abandoned pet cemetery in Nevada reading, "Only a cat, I could not have asked for more."[19]

The first known use of "only a cat" was in 1876, when a book by that title by Mrs. H. H. B. Paull appeared in England. Dedicated to Baroness Angela Burdett-Coutts, president of the Ladies Committee of the Royal Society for the Prevention of Cruelty to Animals, it presented the biography of a housecat named Tom, who served as the story's narrator. The phrase was intended as a jibe at those readers who might initially underestimate Tom's virtues, and this point was driven home from the start: "only a cat" served not only as the title, but also as the subtitle of the first chapter and the start of the introductory sentence:

> "ONLY A CAT."
> CHAPTER 1.
> "ONLY A CAT."
> "Only a cat!" Quite true, gentle reader, and yet I am about to try and interest
> you with the history of my long life. I have more confidence in the attempt
> because I have heard great talk lately of the improved estimation in which
> our race is held by society in general.[20]

Embossed cover of the 1876 first edition of Only A Cat, *along with the title-page image showing Tom, the book's feline narrator, who was not averse to socializing with his family's chickens.*

The book had introduced the phrase, but it was published in London and without an edition in the United States, so "only a cat" was not initially popular among Americans. The hubbub surrounding Fannie Howe's burial pushed "only a dog" to the forefront of public discourse, however, and in the aftermath cat lovers were inspired to claim their own phrase. A great flurry of "only a cat" literature began to appear in the USA, although there was a notable difference in how the phrase was used. "Only a dog" primarily served to memorialize individual pets, but while the "only a cat" verses often did tell of a cat's passing, they tended to do so in a way that framed the real goal, which was a broader discussion of the inhumane treatment of felines.

One such poem that became popular by 1890 was based entirely around the repetition of the phrase. Unattributed, it was composed of three stanzas of four lines each, which told of a stray, crying in an alley, killed by a man who had thrown a bootjack. This was a common way to deal with caterwauling, and since bootjacks were made of iron and had pointed prongs, they often caused fatal injuries. The poem in effect urged gentleness towards strays. Typically, it ran under the headline "A Midnight Murder," an incriminating title that made clear that the verses disparaged those people who might do harm to cats.

> ONLY A CAT IN THE MOONLIGHT,
> ONLY A CAT, THAT'S ALL;
> ONLY A SONG AT MIDNIGHT,
> ONLY A WILD, WEIRD WAUL.
>
> ONLY A MAN IMPULSIVE,
> ONLY A REASON FLOWN;
>
> ONLY A CLUTCH CONVULSIVE,
> ONLY A BOOTJACK THROWN.
>
> ONLY A SUDDEN SALLY,
> ONLY AN UTTERED "SCAT!"
> ONLY A CORPSE IN THE ALLEY,
> ONLY A POOR DEAD CAT. [21]

Another poem, also popular in the 1890s and attributed to Elizabeth Harcourt Mitchell, a writer of modest renown, was titled "Lament of a Forsaken Cat." This was an era in which it was common for people to abandon pets when it became inconvenient to keep them. The verses were placed in the voice of a cat that had been left to starve to death when its family went on vacation, and appealed to readers to honor their commitments to any they had taken in. "Only a cat" served as the conclusion to each of its six stanzas.

The family went out of town,
Refreshing themselves by the sea;
I thought they'd have taken me down,

But no one had pity on me.
  What of that?
After all, it is "only a cat!"

The children got in one by one,
When the carriage drove up to the door.
How breathlessly I did run!
Little Molly cried, "Room for one more!"
  What of that?
After all, it is "only a cat!"

"No place with the children for me?
With the luggage then, porter," I said.
"Get out, little demon," cried he,
And gave me a blow on the head.
  What of that?
After all, it is "only a cat!"

There is no one without or within;
Not a drop, not a crumb in the house.
My bones breaking through my skin;
No strength to say Boo to a mouse!
  What of that?
After all, it is "only a cat!"

I was petted and loved by the fair;
Do they think of me now by the sea?
The pavement is burning and bare,
I am dying by inches, poor me!
  What of that?
After all, it is "only a cat!"

You have left me to die, but I say
That when you have once made a friend,
And loved him a little each day,
You should love him on straight to the end!
  Think of that!
Even should he be, "only a cat!"[22]

MINNIE
Only a cat.
1927 ~ 1937

Urging sympathy towards kittens, another poem, which appeared under the title "The Pussy Mother," used "only a cat" in its first and second stanzas. At the time, spaying and neutering were not practiced, so an alternate and considerably more cruel method of population control became common: drowning an entire litter, or saving only a single kitten as a courtesy to the mother. Even Tom, in the book *Only A Cat*, barely escaped such a fate, selected by his mother cat's human family as the sole survivor of a litter of five.[23] The unattributed verses again placed the situation in the eyes of the cat.

I AM ONLY A CAT,
BUT MOTHERS, YOU SEE,
ARE FOND OF THEIR CHILDREN,
WHATEVER THEY BE.

AND I REALLY MUST SAY,
THOUGH ONLY A CAT,
MY ANXIETY SENDS,
MY HEART PITAPAT!

THOSE DEAR LITTLE KITTIES,
SO FLUFFY AND ROUND,
ARE ALL I POSSESS, FOR
THE OTHERS WERE DROWNED.

ALAS WHO CAN WONDER
I TREMBLE WITH FRIGHT
WHENEVER MY BABIES
ARE OUT OF SIGHT?

OH, IT'S SIMPLY ABSURD
OF PEOPLE TO SAY
THAT POOR PUSSY MOTHERS
DON'T SUFFER THAT WAY!

FOR FIRMLY I DECLARE
MOST SOLEMNLY THAT
A MOTHER'S A MOTHER
IF QUEEN OR A CAT![24]

Another "Only a cat" grave is found at Aspin Hill,
dedicated to Minnie, died 1937.

All of this greatly enriches our understanding of Dewey's gravestone. No doubt Dewey's owner had some familiarity with the "only a cat" genre of literature, and knew that using the phrase on his gravestone would signify to fellow initiates the intimate place he held, that he was considerably more than a mere animal. In addition, it raised a familiar battle cry about the inhumane treatment specifically visited upon cats. This does not get us any closer to knowing who Dewey's owner was, however, or the nature of the grief for which he offered comfort. There is, however, another "only a cat" poem that provides specific clues. Attributed to a Lillian M. Dowse, it is titled "She Loves Me and I Love Her."

> ONLY A PUSSY-CAT, SOFT, WARM AND GRAY,
> AND I HEAR SOME ONE ASK, WHAT OF THAT?
> SHE GAVE ME SUCH COMFORT ON MANY A DAY,
> AND A SWEET LITTLE PUSS SHE WAS, SO THEY SAY,
> WHAT OF THAT? WHAT OF THAT?
> SHE WAS ONLY A CAT.
>
> ONLY A PUSSY-CAT SAT BY MY SIDE,
> AND I HEAR YOU AGAIN, WHAT OF THAT?
> SHE WAS ALWAYS MY FRIEND, WHATEVER BETIDE,
> AND MANY'S THE TROUBLE TO HER I CONFIDE.
> SHE IS ONLY A CAT.
> BUT I SAY, WHAT OF THAT? WHAT OF THAT?
>
> ONLY A PUSSY-CAT'S SOFT LITTLE PURR!
> AND YOU ASK, WHAT OF THAT?
> A BUNDLE OF COSINESS DONE UP IN FUR;
> BUT SHE LOVES ME AND I LOVE HER,
> THOUGH SHE'S ONLY A CAT.
> WHAT OF THAT? WHAT OF THAT?[25]

Muddled by an apparent change in verb tense from the past to the present in the third stanza, the poem is no classic of the genre and was quickly forgotten after its publication. But the first and second stanzas reveal some common ground with Dewey's epitaph. Those sections seem to memorialize a specific feline rather than arguing for humane treatment—unusual enough among "only a cat" poems—plus the animal in question comforts the owner. This is specifically mentioned in the third line of the first stanza, while in the third and fourth lines of the second stanza it is noted that the cat in question remained by the owner's side as a trusted confidant no matter what happened.

This makes "She Loves Me and I Love Her" a potential precedent for the gravestone, and there are additional connections. The poem first appeared in 1903, so during Dewey's lifetime, in *Our Dumb Animals*. The Massachusetts SPCA's journal was readily available in the Boston area, thanks in particular to the city's police department, which had volunteered its services to help with distribution. Whoever buried Dewey presumably had a love of animals, so it is fair to assume that this person was familiar with the local publication and, if so, may have seen the poem. Moreover, the listed author, Lillian M. Dowse, was not who she seemed. The name was a *non de plume*, with the real author being Mrs. Elbridge P. Jones, who happened to be one of the initial directors of the Animal Rescue League of Boston—the very organization that owned the cemetery in which Dewey was buried.[26]

This makes for a compelling case that this specific poem served as an inspiration for the grave's inscription, although we still lack an identity for Dewey's owner. Fortunately, there is a further piece of information with which to work. While it is true that there are no primary sources related to Dewey's life, and that newspaper accounts from the 1920s on offered no information on the story behind the grave, an article about Pine Ridge from the *Boston Globe* in 1915, five years after the burial, included the first ever photo published of Dewey's headstone. And underneath the photo was a caption that mentioned a Mrs. S. E. Stuart in connection with it.[27] This seems at first too good to be true, and it almost is: Stuart was an extremely common family name in New England, so even if the caption is correct there are numerous potential candidates.

Among them, however, is one who would seem an ideal match. She was born under the name Susan Elizabeth Nutting in 1853 in Groton, Massachusetts. Her father was Charles, a Civil War veteran, and her mother was Susan,

Another "Only a Cat," in the Nevada desert, and beloved Tinker, at Happy Woodland in Canada.

OVERLEAF: *The grave of feline fashion plate Frosty Foster, died in 1945 and interred at Aspin Hill.*

for whom she was named. In November 1877, at the age of twenty-four, she married George Allen Stuart, his profession listed as bookkeeper. This of course made her Mrs. S. E. Stuart. They then settled in Boston itself, living in an apartment on Hancock Street. George eventually changed careers and went into the lumber business. They never had children but prospered financially, becoming wealthy enough that, in the 1890s, they were able to give up their apartment and purchase a house on Lanark Road.

It sounds from the outside like a good life, with no harbinger of the loneliness and pain the gravestone mentions. In fact, things were not as well as they seemed. Susan never offered a public comment on her husband's declining condition in the early 1900s, but newspapers were succinct in their appraisal. "It is thought that he has become mentally deranged," is how they put it.[28] Whatever was going wrong with George finally spilled out into the street on April 30, 1903, when he was found convulsing a mile from home. He had overdosed on laudanum, an opiate tincture.

A doctor was called to pump his stomach, and Susan explained that he'd been taking opiates for headaches, insisting that the overdose was simply an accident.[29] But it was no accident when George was discovered five days later lying on his bed with a self-inflicted razor slash to his throat. A doctor was again summoned. The cut was not deep and he survived. We cannot know what, if any, attempts were made to help George, only that he would again attempt suicide on May 17. This time he succeeded, the medical examiner listing the cause of death in a handwritten scrawl: "Suicide by incised wound of throat."[30]

Susan was left a widow, and with no children. The pain she felt must have been immeasurable, as it very likely had been throughout whatever drama behind closed doors had led up to her husband's suicide. In this period of catastrophic grief, did Susan turn to a cat for comfort? And did this cat console her with a seemingly human level of sympathy? Perhaps that is still too great a leap. Having unveiled the true identity of the author of "She Loves Me and I Love Her" as Mrs. Elbridge P. Jones provides us with a further avenue to search for clues, however, since she leads us to the annual reports of the Animal Rescue League of Boston.

Although Mrs. Jones eventually gave up her position as a director, she remained an active member. In 1910, in the same roster in which she was listed as in the role of donor, a new name appears. This was the year Dewey died, and Susan, who had never previously been active in the organization, was listed as having made a five-dollar donation.[31] The next year, the anniversary of Dewey's death, Susan made a twenty-five-dollar donation, with the instruction that the

OVERLEAF: *Images from the Carlisle Kats Klub, a Massachusetts cat sanctuary with a cemetery, plus an epitaph from a cat owner in Helsinki, apologizing for being absent at Mummi's passing.*

Mummi
maaliskuu 1988 – 07.07.2009

Suuri on suru kun en ollut sulkemassa silmiäsi,
suuri on suru kun en saanut kuulla viimeisiä sanojasi.
Suuri on suru kun luotani lähdit,
suuri on suru kun elämäsi uneen hiljaiseen päätit.
Silti uskon jossain syvällä sydämessäni
että sinulla kyyneleet muuttui lopulta iloksesi,
kun kipu ei tehnytkään enää elämääsi helvetiksi.
Sillä enkeli kuuli kaukaa sinun viimeisen rukouksesi
ja vastasi – kyllä, pieni lapseni
minä muutan helvetin
taivaaksesi.

money should go specifically to the Pine Ridge facility where he was buried. A year later, she paid a hundred dollars to purchase a lifetime membership in the league, and in the same year's report another new name appears. A one-dollar associate membership was registered "In Memory of Dewey the Cat."

We can now bring in a final clue. The same article that first published a photo of the grave noted one additional fact: Dewey's owner lived in Boston's Back Bay.[32] At first glance, this is disappointing, since Lanark Street is not located there. But the value of Susan's estate slowly dwindled after George's death, and she was eventually forced to give up the house. Census records show that by the 1910s, when Dewey passed and when the article was published, Susan was living instead on Dartmouth Street—which is exactly in the center of Back Bay.

The pieces align perfectly, the name, dates, geography, tragedy, and increasing donations to the league that governed the cemetery all fit. And if Susan had indeed turned in her pain and loneliness to a cat possessed of the magical ability to comfort, she in recompense offered him a grave with an epitaph inspired by a poem written by a woman who was active in the same organization to which she would immediately start making donations and continue to support financially. And perhaps not coincidentally, this poem appeared the same year in which her husband committed suicide.

Circumstantially, the evidence seems overwhelming, although unless further pieces emerge to prove that Susan owned a cat named Dewey or purchased his burial plot, the world's most famous cat grave will always carry a footnote of mystery. But that may not be so bad after all—perhaps we would miss the point in wanting the story to be told in full. Even as the cracks grow with each passing year and the delicately carved letters are rendered increasingly dim, Dewey's gravestone will continue to speak, regardless of what we know of his life. The beauty of his story is not, in the end, what happened between 1898 and 1910. Its beauty is instead in the way it conjures for everyone who sees it the specter of their own Dewey, the one they once knew, or perhaps now know, the one that was never "only" a pet. That is Dewey's true memorial, and the march of time cannot silence the voice that speaks from his grave. The love he shared speaks eternally.

It is never only a cat: passersby in California offered this roadside grave to an unknown stray.

IV

Death in
Tinsel Town

Wild Tales &

Famous Animals

IV

 ## A Tale of Two Kitties: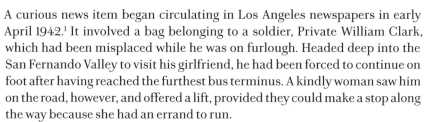
Tawny, Cinderella, and Celebrity Pets

A curious news item began circulating in Los Angeles newspapers in early April 1942.[1] It involved a bag belonging to a soldier, Private William Clark, which had been misplaced while he was on furlough. Headed deep into the San Fernando Valley to visit his girlfriend, he had been forced to continue on foot after having reached the furthest bus terminus. A kindly woman saw him on the road, however, and offered a lift, provided they could make a stop along the way because she had an errand to run.

That was fine by Private Clark, although unfortunately he forgot to retrieve the bag containing his shirts, socks, and other sundries from the trunk of her car. He had a reasonable excuse for the oversight, since the errand had created such an air of confusion as to leave him temporarily absent-minded, and local editors took pity, eager to help a fellow in uniform. It shouldn't be too hard to identify the woman in question, they assumed, given the particulars of the story. Did anyone know someone named Mary who might have given a ride to a soldier while en route to the local pet cemetery to place flowers on the grave of her lion?

In most cities, such a news item would have seemed bizarre, perhaps an April Fool's prank. But not in Los Angeles, where weird was the norm when it came to animal burials. Indeed, it wasn't hard to find the woman. Not only had she gained considerable notoriety thanks to an often pitched battle to keep a full-grown, male lion in a suburban neighborhood, the animal himself had been familiar in Hollywood circles as a working screen actor. In addition, the story behind his grave was one of the best known and most poignant that the Los Angeles Pet Memorial Park had to offer.[2]

Tawny the Lion was born in 1918 to a circus, the owners of which were not kind to their animals, and he wound up neglected and abused. That Tawny's tale did not turn as tragic as Goldfleck's was entirely due to Mary McMillan, who took him in as a rescue and nursed him back to health. In the process, she developed an emotional bond that bordered on maternal instinct. As an adult, Tawny awed strangers as a fearsome beast, but he remained forever Mary's little boy, and she dedicated the rest of her life to his service. Of course, there would be considerable challenges in raising him, not the least of which was finding a place where they could live.

When Mary first acquired Tawny, he was small enough to sleep at the foot of her bed. But as he eventually grew towards seven feet long, she received an ultimatum: her landlord informed her that she must choose between the lion and the house. Mary did not hesitate. She chose Tawny. With eviction looming

and the very real possibility that Los Angeles might see a lion on skid row, they were saved by the Jack London Club, a charity that helped animals rescued from circuses and zoos. The club arranged for the purchase of a home on Chandler Boulevard, and Mary's fortunes further improved as word spread of her efforts to keep Tawny as a pet. There was no shortage of work in Hollywood for a gentle giant like him, a big, exotic cat who was domesticated enough to safely interact with people. The movie studies came calling, offering parts in films, and before long it was he who was paying the bills.

Tawny's filmography is difficult to reconstruct. Animal actors were not usually credited unless they were playing lead roles, but his most prominent appearances were in the Tarzan movies starring Johnny Weissmuller. And while he never rose above cameos, he did manage to score the most famous cameo of all: Leo, the MGM lion. The trademark role, shown at the start of all the studio's films, was introduced in 1916 and played by many different animals. Tawny was among those that the studio periodically hired for the spot, making him a legitimate piece of Hollywood history.

Unfortunately, the lion's growing celebrity status did not assuage the neighbors, who had long held trepidations about living next to a 450-pound predator. They forced Mary before a judge, initially with a complaint about disturbing the peace due to Tawny's habit of letting out mighty roars in the still of the night. They then tacked on a charge of keeping a dangerous animal without a license. Mary was especially irate about the latter. In truth, she was considerably more fierce than Tawny, and convinced a sympathetic judge that her lion was no more threat than a pussycat. He was allowed to stay, and the chagrined neighbors would simply have to put up with the late-night roars.

But vindication in court still did not solve all of Tawny's troubles. It would take another feline to do that, because as much love as Mary could give, he was a lonely lion, the only one of his kind in the urban jungle. Which brings us back to his grave, and why it is so special: it is not a resting place for him alone. Tawny's companion in death arrived unexpectedly one summer's day, having strolled onto the property unannounced. He may have thought himself big enough under normal circumstances, being a tomcat of large stature, although he was

As a Hollywood lion, Tawny picked up odd jobs like this for films and photo shoots.

dwarfed by his distant feline cousin. But this didn't bother the visitor, as he and Tawny found that they had quite a lot in common. They were both cats, even if drastically different types, both had come to Mary in search of a home, and both needed a friend.

The tomcat decided to move in, which was fine by the lion, and Mary named their new housemate Cinderella. It was a curiously feminine sobriquet for a tomcat, but he didn't seem to mind. Maybe he understood that, in Tawny, he had found a prince, and the bromance that would unfold between them was a fairytale of the most unusual sort. Hollywood's original odd couple, they were inseparable, lounging together in the grass under the warm California sun during the day, and huddled together at night, with the tomcat wrapped in the lion's paws, which were nearly as big as he. And this Cinderella's coach was no pumpkin, but rather Tawny himself, as he perched upon his big buddy's back and dug in with his claws to ride around the yard—begging the question of which of them was the real King of the Beasts.

Indeed, the tomcat certainly acted like he was in charge. He watched over his larger cousin with a keen eye, and his concern for the lion was such that, when dental problems left Tawny to subsist on a diet of oatmeal, Cinderella tended his dignity by licking away loose gobs from his snout and whiskers as if he were but a kitten. In each other's company the pair had found something that no human could provide, and they stayed by each other's side, even as the sun set on their golden years. Time finally claimed its due in 1939, with Cinderella the first victim. It was said that Tawny's demeanor changed afterward, and he himself did not last much longer. Depressed and pining for his companion, he died on February 8, 1940.

Mary, who had devoted her life to Tawny's well-being, would provide for him in death as well, sparing no expense on his grave. She chose a plot for him atop a hill, at the highest point of the Los Angeles Pet Memorial Park, providing a magnificent view over the rolling fields below. A huge granite marker, among the largest on the grounds, was ordered in his memory. "With malice toward none he bore the adversities of his life with mankind," began the inscription. It was a fitting epitaph for a kindly lion who started out as an abused cub and had known nothing other than the city as his home.

Friends to the end: the inset photo of Cinderella on Tawny's back marks their shared grave.

1918   1940

"TAWNY"   AFRICAN LION

WITH MALICE TOWARD NONE, HE BORE THE
ADVERSITIES OF HIS LIFE WITH MANKIND.
GENTLE, LIFELONG PROTECTOR OF HIS ADORED
TOMCAT PAL, WHO SLEEPS BESIDE HIM HERE.
BELOVED, ALWAYS FAITHFUL COMPANIONS OF
MARY MCMILLAN WHO REARED THEM
TOGETHER WITH LOVING KINDNESS.

In Hollywood, Tawny had never risen above a bit player, but his imposing grave made him a star, better known in death than in life, as people retold the story of the movie lion buried in the pet cemetery. Indeed, it had become such a part of local lore that when the remarkable tale caused Private Clark to forget his bag, local newspaper editors had no doubt that among their readers, someone would be familiar enough with it that they could help locate Mary. But those who looked more closely at the grave would see that the lion was only half the story—it was Cinderella's resting place too. Tawny had entered Mary's life sad and lonely, and as her final service on his behalf, she would make sure he did not exit that way.

When Cinderella passed, he was given a temporary burial in Mary's yard, from which he was then exhumed so that the pair could be reunited, the two felines finding their final rest as they had spent the latter parts of their lives, alongside one another. Tawny was the "gentle, lifelong protector of his adored tomcat pal who sleeps beside him here," continued the inscription. And inset above the text was a photo, now faded but still discernable, showing them together, Cinderella perched proudly upon Tawny's back. Two stray cats who in life had found their greatest joy in each other's company, now together for eternity.

That it was a perfectly scripted ending is perhaps no surprise since the Los Angeles Pet Memorial Park is Hollywood's pet cemetery. It was here that the companions of the most famous stars of the silver screen were laid to rest,

and many of them were even celebrities in their own right. The grounds were dotted with stories that no other animal burial ground could match, stories like Tawny's that were as touching as they were weird, and infused with the magnetic appeal of Hollywood. And it was this combination, in an increasingly celebrity-obsessed culture, that made it the most famous pet cemetery in the world within a decade of its founding in 1928.

The obsession with celebrity animals and animals owned by celebrities was not new, however. It dated all the way back to the first pet cemeteries. Even Hyde Park boasted of a celebrity pet: although the graves there were almost exclusively for the animals of aristocrats, one had been set aside for Pompey, a dog owned by Florence St. John, the leading star of the music halls in Victorian and Edwardian England. And Pompey himself was said to have acted, presumably alongside his mistress. Celebrity burials have always been considered notable, they were the ones pointed out as a kind of imprimatur that confirmed the grounds were special.

American pet cemeteries in particular always seem to have some kind of connection to celebrity. Not surprisingly, Hartsdale early on became the burial ground for the pets owned by the big Broadway stars. One of the cemetery's first prominent clients was Irene Castle, who together with her husband, Vernon, ushered in the dance craze of the early 20th century by appearing in wildly popular Broadway shows and silent films. Irene buried several pets at Hartsdale, among them her monkey Rastas, "The smartest, most lovable monkey that ever lived," and "My beloved Zowie," a dog given the touching epitaph, "I do not cringe from death so much / Since you are gone, my truest friend. / Thy dear dumb soul will wait for mine / However long before the end."

Further down the East Coast, Clara Glen Pet Cemetery took in a quirky cadre of performing animals from Atlantic City. They included Rex the Wonder Dog, who in the 1930s gained fame for a waterskiing act, and Parry, a dog who rode along the boardwalk on a tricycle while holding a pipe in his mouth. The latter's impressive grave has now fallen into several pieces but was designed as a stage with theater curtains and comedy and tragedy masks, and inscribed, "Show-biz was his life and love." Further south, in Richmond, Virginia, Pet Memorial Park provided the final resting place for America's most famous psychic horse, Lady Wonder. She was able to spell out answers to questions by turning over letter blocks with her nose, and her powers were esteemed enough that she was consulted by police investigators seeking clues in hard-to-solve cases.

The first pet cemetery in Florida could claim as its big celebrity connection not the animals, but rather the man who interred them. Colonel Tom Parker, who later gained fame as Elvis Presley's manager, had once been employed in Tampa in the humble role of dog catcher. Among his responsibilities was managing the cemetery operated by the local SPCA, and the office still has receipts for plots bearing his signature. Elvis himself is meanwhile depicted on the grave of a beagle named Tippy at Hinsdale Animal Cemetery, having sung "Hound Dog" to the animal on stage at Chicago Stadium in 1972.

Aspin Hill claims bragging rights to a very big name, with the grave of one of the most familiar animal stars from Golden Age Hollywood. Petey, the black-and-white bulldog who appeared with a circle drawn around one eye

Pompey, was the first celebrity pet burial; Rex was famous in Atlantic City for riding an aquaboard.

OVERLEAF: *Broadway star Irene Castle had a plot at Hartsdale for pets ranging from dogs to monkeys.*

IRENE CASTLE (1893–1969)
Renowned dancer and animal welfare
advocate kept a menagerie of pets that
accompanied her as she performed
throughout the world.

Between 1917 and 1924
she buried her beloved pets on this site,
including a monkey, a Bulldog Terrier mix
and five Brussels Griffons.

"A piece of my heart is buried here"
– I. C.

in the *Our Gang* (*Little Rascals*) comedies. Petey isn't actually there, however. The long-standing rumor that he is buried at Aspin Hill is due to a grave for a similar-looking dog named General Grant, aka Jiggs, whose headstone noted him as an "RKO dog." People assumed the inscription was a reference to RKO Pictures, hence the *Our Gang* connection, but in fact the RKO in question was a kennel.[3]

Of course, any Hollywood insider would immediately realize how wildly off base the wishful thinkers in Maryland were. The *Our Gang* comedies were made by Hal Roach Studios, not RKO! As for Petey, or the Peteys, since there were more than one, they were buried at Los Angeles Memorial, which is hardly a surprise since that's where the most famous animals are all buried. It is the only pet cemetery that prints a star map as a guide to the grounds, and it is the only one that has a justifiable reason to do so. Everywhere else has always paled in comparison to "The Valhalla of dogs and cats of the screen," as it was dubbed, or alternately, "Hollywood's amazing cemetery for pets of stars."[4]

The cemetery's reputation belies the fact that the pets of Southern California's more mundane citizens have always vastly outnumbered those of celebrities within its grounds. It is in most respects a typical pet cemetery: there are, for instance, memorials that tug at the heartstrings, charming displays of whimsy, and epitaphs from grieving owners that probably didn't come out exactly the way they intended. You wouldn't have known it from the press, however. Newspaper accounts dangled every famous name who had buried a pet there, making it sound as if strolling the grounds was like playing hopscotch along the Hollywood Walk of Fame.

Readers ate up the stories about celebrities and their animals, and it wasn't just for the gossip. Residents of the workaday world might not have shared much in common with the glittering royalty that held court in their neighborhood movie houses, but they did find common ground in the ineffable grief of pet loss. Fame could not shield a person from that distress, and accounts of broken-hearted stars made them somehow more tangible, like gods turned mortal by the death of a beloved dog or cat. And that grief had become an increasingly complex issue in Los Angeles as the city transformed from a Wild West cow town to a media metropolis.

Not only was there no designated space for animal burials, the city council even passed an ordinance specifically prohibiting pet cemeteries.[5] The interment of pets in residential areas of the city was meanwhile illegal, and it was a restriction the local police had traditionally been known to enforce. This left the newly minted stars of the silver screen not only to face the emotional

---

PREVIOUS: *Not so famous: this grave has often been misidentified as that of Petey from the* Little Rascals.

Lacking a cemetery, Los Angeles residents had to improvise: a backyard burial for a cat from the 1940s.

trauma of a pet's death, but in a quandary when it came to disposing of the body since, as public figures, they had to use added discretion lest their actions be gossiped upon. Many stories dating from this era take on extra tragedy owing to the inability to provide a permanent memorial for historically important animals. A prime example is Mutt, an early canine actor who starred alongside Charlie Chaplin in *A Dog's Life*.

Chaplin had written the film with the intention of producing and directing it as the first offering from his newly founded studio. The script was the story of a faithful dog that digs up a hidden coin purse, thereby providing enough money to transform the life of his human friend, a tramp, from pauper to prince. But this was 1917, before the era of the big-name animal actors, and Chaplin was in a bind: unless he could find the right canine sidekick, he had no film. Then he discovered Mutt, a mixed-breed mongrel, in the city pound.[6] The decision to cast Mutt smacks of equal parts intuition and desperation. Chaplin was trusting a dog who was entirely untrained for stage or screen not only with his production, but potentially with his career: if the film failed, it could cost the actor both his studio and his professional standing. Mutt loved people, however, and was determined to do his best for the man who had rescued him. He wished to please, but even so he often became nervous on set since interacting with humans so closely and under such scrutiny was entirely new to him.

The crew adored the sweet little dog and developed various means to calm him when he appeared anxious—including offering sips of whiskey—and Mutt completed the film with results beyond what anyone could have dreamed. Released in 1918, *A Dog's Life* was Chaplin's biggest success to date. It was in effect an early blockbuster, serving as a stepping stone for even bigger things to come, and proving that his studio was a viable entity. As for the actor's

Mutt died a star, acting alongside Charlie Chaplin,
but his fame could not secure a permanent memorial.

own role, that of the tramp, it was so popular with audiences that it became a signature character the actor would replay in some of the most famous early Hollywood films.

Mutt had gone from the city pound to movie star in one fell swoop. In recompense for the extraordinary service he had rendered, he was appointed as a goodwill ambassador for the studio. The once homeless dog had a forever home there, roaming the grounds as he wished and bringing smiles to the faces of all he met. The life of the dog behind *A Dog's Life* couldn't have seemed more perfect. But Mutt's own script was due for a cruel twist. He was about to meet a tragic end, and his demise came as quickly and unexpectedly as his success.

Soon after finishing the film, Chaplin left Hollywood for a nationwide tour to sell war bonds. Mutt suddenly began to panic. Everyone at the studio doted over him, so from a human perspective there seemed no need for him to fret. But it was Chaplin he had bonded with, and it was his love for the actor that had allowed him to overcome his trepidations and excel on set. Now Chaplin was gone, and despite the affections of the people around him, the dog began to suffer far worse anxiety attacks than he had experienced during filming. He began wandering the studio, desperately seeking his missing friend, sinking further into depression all the while.

Veterinarians were called in when Mutt began refusing food. None had a prescription for what ailed him, however, since the only cure was Chaplin himself. The studio staff made what was in retrospect a terrible decision. They did not tell the actor that the dog was ailing. Most likely they were afraid of his reaction—he had a legendary temper—and since he was by then near the end of his tour, they gambled that Mutt could hold on. Would Chaplin have returned early had he been apprised? Abandoning a promise to the War Department for the sake of the dog who had offered the actor his heart? We can never know, and the studio staff guessed wrong: Mutt gave up days before the actor's return. His death came less than two months after *A Dog's Life* had premiered.

A poor pooch whose rapid succession of triumph and tragedy was as heart-wrenching as anything Hollywood could dream up certainly deserved a fitting funeral, if not a grand memorial. But in those days there was nowhere to publicly bury him, and there was nothing his or Chaplin's fame could do about it. A grave was surreptitiously dug at the site of his greatest glory, the spot in the studio's yard where the scene of him finding the coin purse had been filmed. His grave would have to be discreet, however, since this was technically an illegal act. Rather than a headstone, it was marked by a humble shoe. Whatever the significance, and we might guess it was an old shoe that he liked to chew on, it bore on its sole the epitaph, "Mutt, died April 29—A broken heart."[7]

The old Chaplin property is now Jim Henson Studios, the shoe is long gone, and the exact location of Mutt's grave, which should be hallowed ground for Hollywood historians, is no longer known. Similar fates have befallen the graves of numerous other early celebrity animals. Pepper, a Mack Sennett Studios cat who scored the first credited role given to a feline, was buried in 1924 somewhere on the old studio lot in Echo Park. It was later converted into a public storage facility, meaning that Hollywood's trailblazing cat may very well lie under a unit containing someone's outdated appliances. And Old Blue, Tom Mix's first movie horse, was interred on the quiet grounds of the actor's ranch, only to later have the clatter of shopping carts disturb his eternal slumber when a supermarket was built on the property.[8] Hollywood's animals needed a cemetery. Fortunately for them, the same man who had been tending their medical needs was preparing to give them one.

Where the Stars Shine Bright: A Pet Cemetery for Los Angeles

Dr. Eugene Jones was known as "the veterinarian to the stars," and he was also something of a star in his own right. Not only did he cater to pets owned by Hollywood's biggest names, he was a true entrepreneur in pet care. His Santa Monica Boulevard animal hospital was better equipped than many hospitals for humans in the 1920s, with its own X-ray facilities, private waiting rooms for VIPs, and a kitchen for preparing meals for pets with special dietary needs. There were even separate surgical bays for cats that prevented them from being bothered by the sights and sounds of dogs. In addition, Dr. Jones offered an impressive portfolio of other services tailored to high-end clients. These included a summer retreat for animals near Big Bear, east of Los Angeles. Pets of the rich and famous could be boarded there in style, taking a break from the city heat in the clean mountain air while their owners traveled the globe.

In effect, Dr. Jones was prepared to take care of his clients' pets from cradle to . . . not quite the grave, but therein lay an opportunity. By the late 1920s, the time was certainly ripe for Los Angeles to get a pet cemetery, and the ambitious veterinarian was well positioned to provide one. Finding the right spot would be no easy feat, however, since it had to be far enough from the metropolitan center to be free from the city's restrictions on animal burials, yet not so far from Hollywood as to seem remote. In addition, since such a cemetery would cater to a high-end clientele, it would have to be at a location that met their tastes,

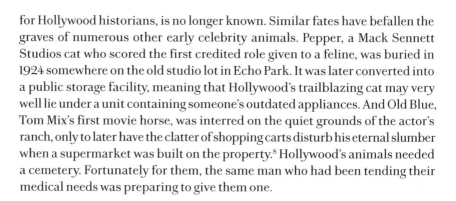

Actress Doris Hill, a starlet at Paramount Pictures, visits the grave of Lucky in 1929 or 1930.

a place with an idyllic feel, but at the same time not somewhere so exclusive as to shut out regular pet owners, who would be the true bread and butter.

Fortuitously, Dr. Jones's brother, Rollins Jones, happened to be a prominent property broker, well connected within the world of Southern California real estate. He would be a partner in the venture, and was able to put together a deal for several acres of land in Calabasas, in the western San Fernando Valley. Calabasas nowadays is the land of McMansions and the Kardashians, but back then it was a sparsely populated cattle grazing area. It was the perfect location, a picturesque setting among rolling hills only fifteen miles to the northwest of Hollywood but feeling a world apart. By the middle of 1928, what would become the Los Angeles Pet Memorial Park had broken ground and begun offering plots.[9]

While the early portents boded well—the initial plot, for instance, went to Dolores del Río, the leading Latin American star of the day—the first year turned out to be a surprisingly bumpy road. It was a Hollywood story to be sure, but one that read more like a gangster movie, very nearly derailing the project from the start. First there was the matter of Moses W. Hornsby, listed as the cemetery's initial president. He himself was something of a name, being the cousin of Rogers Hornsby, one of the greatest baseball players of the day

Among the cemetery's prominent early clients was Mexican-born starlet Dolores del Río.

and an inductee in the Major League Hall of Fame. Moses, on the other hand, found himself headed to the halls of justice soon after interments began in 1929. He had gone to the apartment of his estranged wife to attempt a reconciliation. It was reconciliation at gunpoint, however, and when his wife tried to lock him in a bathroom, he wound up shooting his stepson and the son of the building's owner, and then shot himself in the chest.[10]

Even worse news for the cemetery came when Gilbert Beesemyer, a financier who had invested $23,000 in the project, was revealed to be a con artist of epic proportions. The money had been part of $8 million embezzled from a loan company, and this forced the cemetery under a court-appointed trust amid talk that it might be liquidated during Beesemyer's bankruptcy proceedings. Hollywood's first pet cemetery was getting publicity to be sure, although not the kind it wanted. And if all this weren't enough, the cemetery was sued during its first year for $10,000. Nicola de Pento, a Calabasas man who had patented a mechanical rocking horse for people to sit on while bathing, wanted the money in damages, claiming that the sight of a budding field of pet graves had caused him depression.[11]

Meanwhile, the grounds weren't exactly living up to the glitz to which Dr. Jones aspired. The earliest surviving photo of the cemetery, dating to early 1929, shows the place having a rustic look, with grave markers of painted wood and the word "HAPPY" spelled out behind them in large, crude letters. The initial grave may have been sold to Dolores del Río, but she had yet to inter a pet in it, and the inscriptions that can be deciphered include no big names. The most notable burial was for a dog named Lobo. He had been owned by LAPD Chief James Davis, who would later wind up in a scandal involving a pet when a kinkajou given to him by a friend in Mexico bit off one of his wife's thumbs. But that was still a decade in the future, and about Lobo little is known, although he apparently posed no danger to Mrs. Davis's digits.

The cemetery did not emerge from its cloud of chaos until 1931, when Rollins Jones formed the Los Angeles Pet Cemetery Corporation to take control of the property and pay off its debts. None of the money went to Mr. De Pento, who apparently went on being depressed, while Hornsby, who had survived his self-inflicted gunshot wound, and Beesemyer were reunited in San Quentin Prison. The cemetery's humble appearance had also begun to change by this time. Bringing to the project the same ambitious zeal with which he had approached his other investments, Dr. Jones had begun a series of improvements that would allow him to provide a wider variety of services than any other pet cemetery in the world.

OVERLEAF: *The earliest known image of the grounds (Lobo the police dog is lower right) and a 1929 photo of the building housing the mausoleum with its stained-glass windows of animals.*

A crematorium was built on-site, making the cemetery one of the few to have its own. Dr. Jones followed that with a unique touch: a columbarium containing shelves and private niches for the urns of cremated pets. Modeled after mausoleums found in human cemeteries, the building overlooked the grounds from the property's northern hill and provided a distinguished focal point. It included stained-glass windows that reflected colored light in the shapes of animals, illuminating the interior while providing a charming, lyrical touch. And to further ensure that Hollywood clients made the trek, the brothers opened a satellite office on Hollywood Boulevard. The elite of the film world could make funeral arrangements there, as well as drop off deceased pets, or use it as a meeting place to drive in procession up to Calabasas. And for those who needed transport for a pet's body, there was a special doggie hearse.

Dr. Jones's efforts paid off, and the first wave of prominent clients included the biggest names of the day. Among them was Chaplin—while the cemetery may have come too late for Mutt, his replacement as studio dog, Teddy, was buried there, as was the actor's cat, Boots. John Gilbert, the dashing leading man known as "the great lover," purchased a grave for his German shepherd Topsy on the gentle slope of the west hill, while Corinne Griffith, not only a famed screen actress but also a savvy businesswoman whose personal fortune was estimated at $150 million, had her canine companions Bozo and Black Rider interred nearby. Just down the row was Jerry, a wire terrier owned by the actress Miriam Hopkins. And they just kept coming, the owners of plots in the

oldest section amounting to a who's who of Hollywood from the 1930s through 1950s, including Betty Grable, Gloria Swanson, Lon Chaney, both Abbott and Costello, Alfred Hitchcock, and Lauren Bacall.

Of course, this being Hollywood, it is not surprising that there were some exotic pets mixed in. Mae West was the first to bury a monkey, her gibbon Boogey. Despite his habit of going through her makeup drawer and ransacking her closets, Mae loved Boogey too much to keep him in a cage, and he was allowed free run of her apartment, even sleeping on her bed. Mae ordered an expensive, satin-lined casket for him, but didn't show up for the funeral. Callous? Not quite. For once, the indomitable persona that Mae offered for public consumption failed her. She feared there might be paparazzi present and, struck by grief, decided she couldn't face the cameras—the *only* time she couldn't face a camera, it was said.[12]

Boogey was more than just a pet, however. He was himself a working actor, having appeared alongside Mae in the 1933 film *I'm No Angel*. Like Tawny, he was one of the cemetery's many residents with film credits, some of them extensive. They included Jiggs, Hollywood's leading chimpanzee, who earned a hundred dollars a day on set and was a standing member of the Screen Actors Guild. Dorothy Lamour, his costar in the 1938 production *Her Jungle Love*, attended his funeral, as did longtime friends Bing Crosby and Ray Milland.[13] Hollywood's leading horse was buried here as well. Topper was almost as familiar to audiences as his rider, Hopalong Cassidy, with sixty-six motion pictures to his name and more screen time than any other equine actor in history.

Teddy lived at Chaplin Studios in the 1930s and 1940s, alongside the resident cat, his friend Topaze.

Dorothy Lamour costarred with Jiggs the chimp and was one of the celebrities who attended his funeral.

TOPPER
HOPALONG CASSIDY'S
HORSE

There were also several show-business birds, including a grave for a talking parakeet named Moira who had played in the 1937 swashbuckling adventure *The Buccaneer*, directed by Cecil B. DeMille. Moira's story is among the most weirdly tragic of any of the animals in the cemetery. Taught by an unknown crewmember to say, "Yes, Mr. DeMille," she began repeating the phrase incessantly. The director was fine with a cadre of yes-men but found a yes-bird to be more than he could take, and Moira was banished from the set. While she was waiting to be removed, however, a carriage hauling a prop cannon rolled loose. Stagehands rushed to grab the runaway artillery but were too late to stop it, and the crew could only look on in horror as it ran right over her cage. DeMille, hoping to quell potential suspicions that the bird's demise was the result of ill will between them, ordered a coffin be custom crafted and a funeral arranged at his expense.[14]

The cemetery also provided the final resting place for Puzzums, Hollywood's second feline star. When Pepper died in 1924, she had left Sennett Studios with a problem beyond the lack of a proper burial place. Up until that time, she had been the only cat who could legitimately act, and was popular with audiences to boot. The studio bosses needed to somehow come up with another acting cat. This could have been a difficult task, but their star found them, having shown up on the lot when an aspiring actress named Nadine Dennis came for an audition and just so happened to have little Puzzums in her handbag.

Nadine, who had discovered Puzzums as an abandoned kitten, tended to be overly protective. She apologized for his presence; the poor boy had been ill, she explained, and she didn't want to leave him home alone. The casting director didn't mind in the least, however. In fact, he had some good news, he just might have a part available. No, not for Nadine, but rather for the cat, who happened to be of an almost identical dark gray color to Pepper. A highly capable learner who had already mastered several tricks taught to him by Nadine, Puzzums was soon on the payroll. Nadine found her charity towards an ailing kitten amply rewarded when, in the end, it was he who was supporting her: Puzzums's exclusive contract with Sennett paid him $250 a week to work alongside such big names as Maurice Chevalier and Jeanette MacDonald, while

Nadine never rose above an extra's rate of $7.50 a day.

Puzzums became Hollywood's new favorite feline until his ladder to the stars collapsed in 1934. First came an accident on set. Exactly what happened has never been fully explained, but he was nearly electrocuted. The ever-protective Nadine thereafter announced him retired. But filthy lucre proved too great a temptation, and several months later she was enticed into allowing him a final role. Puzzums wound up cast alongside Will Rogers in a picture called *Handy Andy* but was forced to suspend filming due to an infection caused by an ulcerated tooth.

Strike that. The story of Puzzums's disappearance from the set soon changed to something considerably more dramatic, with the trade papers reporting that the valiant cat was struggling against venom delivered by the bite of a black widow spider.[15] Whichever version one chooses to believe—although it seems clear that the publicists at Sennett had concocted the spider bite as a story with more pizazz—the end result was the same. Puzzums died on August 18, and was buried the next afternoon in a plot near the top of the hill. On the same day as his death, Nadine received a call from the Humane Society, telling her that Puzzums had been selected to receive a gold medal in thanks for his appearances at fundraisers for local animal shelters. Unaware of his passing, the society had hoped that a gala ceremony might be arranged to present his medal. Instead it was awarded in a somber service at his graveside.

Despite the cat's dour end, Nadine was proud enough of Puzzums's role in Hollywood history to purchase a gravestone that proclaimed him "A Sennett Cat." Or at least that's what it said in the 1930s, as was widely attested to at the time. The stone eventually vanished, leaving his plot an empty patch of grass. Did it fall victim to the cat's own fame, perhaps stolen by a fan or movie buff? The suspicion may explain why some celebrities never purchased grave markers for their pets. Mae West, for instance, never provided one for Boogey, and several other prominent burials are in unmarked plots. This might otherwise seem surprising, since these were people of means who tended to dote upon their animals. But it may be that some celebrities, being well acquainted with the behavior of fans, decided that secrecy was the best guardian of their pets' graves.

As Hollywood's leading horse, Topper worked with Hopalong Cassidy for over two decades.

Pictured with his owner, Nadine Dennis, Puzzums went from stray to star as Hollywood's favorite cat.

The perils of fame for a Hollywood animal could reach far beyond stolen headstones, however. In fact, in the case of one movie dog, his celebrity status cost him his life. Dumpsie was of uncertain breed, variously described as a Maltese, a Yorkie, or an Australian Silky. He is almost completely forgotten now, but in his heyday in the early 1930s he was a much-loved canine actor who tallied several film roles. These included such major productions as *Palmy Days*, a musical comedy starring Eddie Cantor and choreographed by Busby Berkeley that was a box office hit in 1931.

But that was only part of the story. The tiny dog had the "it" factor. Spunky, affectionate, and with a true zest for life, it was said that Dumpsie could do anything but card tricks. And maybe that was true: when a special canine games was held in conjunction with the 1932 Los Angeles Olympics, he shocked the field by bringing home the gold in the hurdles despite his diminutive size.[16] Lionel Barrymore, an animal lover who had himself buried a dozen pets at the Los Angeles Pet Memorial Park, offered the then princely sum of $5,000 for the dog, although Dumpsie's owner, Bonnie Ferguson, declined the offer.

As it turned out, not quite everyone loved Dumpsie. Not the anonymous person who telephoned Bonnie on the morning on November 12, 1934, to offer a dire warning: Dumpsie would be dead by nightfall, he said, and then hung up. Bonnie was dumbfounded. She and Dumpsie were set to do a radio spot that afternoon, but now she had cause for alarm. It must be a mean-spirited prank, she reasoned. After all, who would want to hurt her little dog? She decided to go ahead with the interview, and all was fine—until afterward, when they were driving out of the parking lot to return home, and an unknown person pushed through a crowd near the gate and tossed a meatball into an open window of the car. Dumpsie greedily gobbled it down, and within hours the cruel prophesy had rung true.[17]

Seven years old and with a promising career ahead of him, Dumpsie was dead. A poisoned meatball had sent a beloved dog to a grave in Calabasas, where he was laid to rest among a crowd of admirers still in shock over the senseless cruelty. Flowers for the funeral were provided by Dumpsie's former castmate Eddie Cantor, devastated by the death of a dog he had come to know as a friend. The *Los Angeles Times*, meanwhile, ran an editorial that verged on a diatribe, with Dumpsie's passing declared a tragedy for the public, who would now be deprived of his talents. The author railed against people who would harm innocent animals. When it came to beasts, he concluded, it is they who are the lowest of all.[18] Yet none of this sentiment, as heartfelt as it was, could provide a who or why to explain the awful act. There were plenty of theories, from an insane fan to rival dog owners, but the police failed to come up with a single suspect, and whoever threw Dumpsie his final, fatal treat escaped justice.

Things like assassination by meatball just didn't happen outside of Hollywood, and stories like Dumpsie's, no matter how tragic they might be, were why Los Angeles's pet cemetery had such a unique allure. But nothing caught the public's fancy quite like the saga of a Doberman pinscher named Kabar. Loyal in life, and at least equally loyal in death, he was the perfect headline attraction: not only was his story the wildest the cemetery had to offer, he had been owned by the biggest star of all, Rudolph Valentino.[19]

Kabar had been the gift of an admiring Belgian diplomat, and it wasn't long before he and Valentino were bonded. A constant companion, the dog was even given the honor of sharing his master's bed, much to the consternation of Valentino's second wife, Natacha Rambova, who felt he preferred the dog to her (a charge Valentino never denied). Even so, they were not entirely inseparable, and when the heartthrob actor traveled to New York in August 1926, he left Kabar behind at Falcon Lair, his Hollywood estate, in the care of his brother Alberto. He felt no need to take the dog across country for what was to be a brief trip, a decision that would hardly have seemed memorable until, separated by three thousand miles, tragedy befell them both.

On August 15, Valentino collapsed at the Hotel Ambassador and was rushed to the New York Polyclinic, where he underwent emergency surgery for appendicitis and gastric ulcers. His prognosis initially seemed promising, but he soon developed pleuritis in his left lung and fell into a coma, dying on the night of August 23. Meanwhile, back in California, Kabar knew something dreadful had happened. He began to cry, a pitiful howl so loud it was audible from the street. Among those who heard his banshee's wail was the actress Beatrice Lillie as she was driving past the house, and it shocked her enough that she nearly drove off the road. Kabar seemed to have gone mad and Alberto had absolutely no idea why. Then word arrived of what the dog already knew, that his master was dead.

Until that time, Kabar had simply been another celebrity's pet, although that alone was noteworthy when the celebrity happened to be Rudolph Valentino. But the events of August 23 laid the first plank in a mythology so occult that Kabar would become a legend in his own right. How could he have known Valentino had died? The dog must have been psychic, people insisted. If he

Perky little Dumpsie's life eventually ended in tragedy, with no charges in his murder ever being brought.

was, however, his powers failed him in the next stage of his mythos, the great wandering, because he left Falcon Lair in an attempt to locate a master who was not to be found in this world.

Details of his quest are murky since none but Kabar knows how far he traveled. Some enthusiastic reporters claimed that he must have carried his quest all the way to New York, although all anyone knew for certain was that he had disappeared. And when he returned several months later, he was not the same Kabar. He seemed a shell of his former self, and not just because of the ardors of his futile journey. His tattered paws would heal and his belly could be filled, but the real loss stemmed from within. He seemed to be a body devoid of a spirit.

For the next year Kabar stood fast, perhaps holding onto some fading glimmer of hope, but after that time came a slow and inexorable demise. He finally passed on January 17, 1929. Alberto selected for his plot a prime location along the road that runs through the lower part of the cemetery and ordered an over-sized headstone inscribed, "Kabar, My Faithful Dog, Rudolph Valentino, Owner." The epitaph was true enough, as the dog had faithfully carried his grief unto death. Kabar's burial did not mark the end of his saga, however, but rather the beginning of an even stranger chapter.

The grave quickly became a pilgrimage site, although the object of veneration was not Kabar himself, but rather Valentino. Since the actor's death, droves of fans had been flocking to his grave, and now they began showing up at his dog's. It seemed to be a test of dedication: anyone could shed a tear for Valentino in the mausoleum at Hollywood Forever Cemetery, but if you were a true fan you would do the same for Kabar. Among the devotees was a mysterious woman, her face obscured by a veil, who looked as if she

Valentino had owned other dogs, but his relationship with Kabar was always felt to be special. Special enough that, according to Hollywood legend, it has endured even beyond the grave.

were floating thanks to a long black dress that fell all the way to the ground. She never spoke a word, and although no one knew her identity she wasn't exactly a stranger. Already famous for keeping a vigil at Valentino's grave, she had become a topic of considerable discussion as the mysterious "woman in black." Now this phantom was appearing at the pet cemetery as well, where she would regularly lay a single lily upon Kabar's headstone.

Kabar himself had apparently still not found peace. There were sightings of his ghost at Falcon Lair, and mediums who attempted to make contact with Valentino in the great beyond sometimes met his Doberman instead. In one case, on May 6, 1948, a phantom dog conforming to Kabar's appearance was said to have jumped through a window and then disappeared.[20] Most frequently, however, he has been reported to haunt the cemetery grounds, with people claiming to have heard or felt the presence of a dog near his headstone. Kabar, it is said, might variously announce himself through muted whimpers or exhaled breaths, brushes against the leg, or even the sensation of licks upon the hand, but when the visitor looks down, there is nothing to be seen.

Parapsychologists assert that the dog's unquiet spirit still grieves, and has remained behind in the hopes of finding Valentino somewhere on the earthly plane. Whether the haunting stories are credible is up to each individual to decide, but what is certain is that they have made Kabar far more famous in death than he was in life. His place in history is now secured, not only as the beloved dog of the silver screen's most celebrated icon, but also as Hollywood's most famous canine phantom—and still, after more than ninety years, among the premier attractions in any pet cemetery.

This monument is dedicated to the memory of the
beloved Toto from the 1939 film, "The Wizard Of Oz."
After the death of Toto, originally named Terry, in 1945,
Owner and Trainer Carl Spitz buried the Cairn Terrier on
his ranch in Studio City. The 1958 construction of the
Ventura Freeway destroyed her resting place.

In Memory of

TOTO

The Supporting Cast:
Some Unlikely Stars

The Los Angeles Pet Memorial Park didn't get all of Hollywood's animals. Some among the high and mighty were given simple backyard interments, including Terry, the cairn terrier who played Toto in *The Wizard of Oz*. She was laid to rest at the home of her trainer, Carl Spitz, in Studio City in 1945, and while her spirit may have traveled Over the Rainbow, her body became forever set in place when the property was razed in 1958 for construction of the Hollywood Freeway. Cars now speed by above her gravesite, which is trapped under tons of concrete. Another of the big names that got away was Pal, a rough collie cast in 1943 as the lead in MGM's *Lassie Come Home*. He would go on to star in six more films before his sons—all of them playing a female role—carried on the franchise as a long-running television show. Pal likewise stayed home, given a burial on the property of his trainer, Rudd Weatherwax.

And since monopoly never goes unchallenged, it was inevitable that competing local pet cemeteries would be founded. Pet Haven opened in 1947 in Gardena, about the same distance south of the civic center as Calabasas is to the northwest. The new cemetery succeeded in siphoning off some A-list burials, including animals owned by Edward G. Robinson and Nat King Cole, while Jerry Lewis buried so many pets that he has an entire section. There was also a "talking chihuahua" that had appeared on *The Ed Sullivan Show*, and the new cemetery even scored Los Angeles's "Dog Number One," Skippy. Said to have been a crossbreed between a German shepherd and a coyote, he had served heroically in World War II, saving the life of his handler at the Battle of Guadalcanal. Upon his return, Mayor Fletcher Bowron officiated a ceremony at City Hall to present Skippy with dog license number one, an honor that marked him as foremost among Los Angeles's canine residents.

Skippy scored another first after his death, one that drew national attention to the new burial ground. Rudd Weatherwax may have preferred to keep Pal out of a pet cemetery, but he had no quarrel with sending one of his famous dog's sons to a ceremony in one if it brought a little publicity. In 1957, Lassie Junior appeared at Skippy's graveside with a throng of reporters and a military color guard to posthumously present the inaugural "Lassie Gold Award." A silver dollar–sized bronze medal, the award was invented as part of a promotion to honor those dogs whose extraordinary actions confirmed their role as

Terry, star of The Wizard of Oz, *is honored at*
Hollywood Forever but his real grave was destroyed.

"man's best friend," while at the same time keeping the Lassie brand circulating in the newspapers.

In addition to the medal, the television show's producers provided Skippy with a gravestone—branded with the Lassie name, of course. Originally, Skippy's burial site had been marked simply by a wooden cross, with painted black letters spelling out "US Army" and "LA 1." But as part of the ceremony, a new marker was placed, inscribed "Skippy, A War Hero, From Lassie," with copies of the front and back of the medal embedded in its face. A hero's burial was effectively turned into an advertisement for a television show, and Lassie Junior's handlers didn't miss the opportunity to get press photos of him deferentially laying a paw on Skippy's headstone as the soldiers stood at attention.[21]

The new cemetery also offered wild and tragic stories that could rival those of its predecessor, such as the saga of Mickey Junior, an English bulldog owned by Mickey Cohen, the mob boss whose life story inspired the 2013 film *Gangster Squad*. A sweet dog in too deep with the wrong crowd, Mickey Junior was on one occasion taken into custody by the LAPD as a witness to a murder. On another, he was stolen and recovered after a high-speed pursuit across Hollywood that included exotic dancers and an actor from *The Beverly Hillbillies*. At the tender age of three, he was run down by a car in West Los Angeles in an apparent hit while out for a walk, his life cut tragically short as a consequence of his association with a human who was by far the less tame of the two.[22] Mickey Junior's funeral at Pet Haven, which included a cadre of FBI agents surveilling the proceedings, was said to be the only time anyone had seen Mickey Senior cry.

Other pet cemeteries would later open in the surrounding counties, and all of them would attract celebrity clients, whose pets are now spread across Southern California. Even in Desert Hot Springs, about a hundred miles east of Los Angeles, there are a surprising number of A-listers at a decidedly humble pet cemetery where a caretaker lives in a trailer and the surrounding sands constantly threaten to overtake the grounds. These burials are due to the proximity of the celebrity enclave in Palm Springs, and they include Liberace's poodles—although searching for them is fruitless unless one knows that the flamboyant pianist kept his identity hidden by listing his name as "Lee" on their

A flag still flies at the grave of Los Angeles's "Dog Number One," the war hero Skippy.

Grumpy Cat left behind millions of social media followers and eight registered trademarks.

headstones. This was apparently an attempt to maintain some anonymity and prevent people from defiling his dogs' graves in search of the diamond-studded collars they were famed for wearing.

The same small cemetery even manages to trump its rivals for patriotism with the grave of Liberty, a golden retriever owned by President Gerald Ford. Hers is a rare burial indeed. Not only is she one of the few First Dogs buried in a pet cemetery, she is the only dog to have ever given birth in the White House, which at the time made her a media sensation. The pet cemetery network kept expanding eastward, eventually crossing the state line into Arizona, and the celebrity burials followed. Sunland Pet Rest opened as a pendant to Sunland Memorial Park in Sun City in 1995, providing an adjacent ground for animal burials. The pet cemetery there has always been small, but it nevertheless drew one of the most famous names in feline history: Grumpy Cat, real name Tardar Sauce, whose dour face attracted millions of social media followers and graced over a thousand licensed products.

A tribute left by a fan on the grave of Prego, the best-known of Liberace's dogs.

OVERLEAF: *Room 8 earned fame as the resident cat at Elysian Heights Elementary School.*

Despite the increasing competition, Los Angeles Pet Memorial Park remains the primary burial choice for the Hollywood elite, even as it approaches its centennial. The cemetery staff does not give out information on the identities of its current clients, but it is well known that the roster includes names that could easily rival the guest list of any Oscars party. Meanwhile, the grounds themselves have made curious stars of a few animals with more pedestrian backgrounds. These include a school cat named Room 8, after the classroom in which he first appeared as a stray at Elysian Heights Elementary in the Echo Park district of Los Angeles. He spent sixteen years as the school's mascot, teaching love and loyalty to its students. Devotion to the cat was such that, on his passing in 1968, enough money was donated to purchase not only a plot for him, but a gravestone so large that it nearly rivals Tawny's. And that devotion has not waned—Room 8 knew thousands of children, and now as adults their continued trips to offer their respects have ensured that it is he, rather than any of the celebrity pets, whose grave is the cemetery's most visited.

But the most unlikely attraction is a one-of-a-kind burial from 1978 that gave the grounds an additional honor that no other pet cemetery in the world can claim: that of an artist's canvas.[23] Blinky the Friendly Hen was already

*A final glimpse: woman mourning her dog Spot,
awaiting burial at Pet Haven in the 1970s.*

dead by the time Jeffrey Vallance, a conceptual artist who later gained some fame as a champion of Tiki culture and for performing a series of séances to summon Richard Nixon's ghost, acquired her. She had been purchased from the butcher's section of a local supermarket as a frozen and headless Foster Farms fryer chicken, and in choosing her as a pet, Vallance hoped to expose the hypocrisy in the way society views animals.

While some are lovingly treated as family members, others are callously killed and eaten, or their bodies used as fodder for industrial purposes. Western culture likes to keep these categories tidy and separate, and seldom questions the disparities, but Vallance knew that the truth was not so simple. We tend to look at only one end of the spectrum, but many animals can be both beloved pets and a potential food source, with the choice being culturally specific and, in many ways, arbitrary. As an example, he had been raised in a society where eating dogs would be considered reprehensible, yet in some parts of the world they are an acceptable meal.

Unfortunately, Vallance's time with his new pet was doomed from the start, since Blinky had already begun to thaw by the time he had gotten her home. Faced with the dilemma of whether he should attempt to prolong their relationship, perhaps by means of refrigeration, or take the more humane (and practical) alternative of releasing Blinky to eternity, Vallance decided to say goodbye. With a heavy heart, he placed his headless companion in a shoebox and drove to the Los Angeles Pet Memorial Park, where he explained to the office staff that he would like to arrange an interment for a hen. A burial for a chicken in and of itself is not a particularly strange request. They are by no means common pets, but they are also not entirely unusual. Many people own them, even in urban environments, so up to this point there was no reason for the staff to expect this was anything out of the ordinary.

That changed, however, when Vallance asked that Blinky be laid out in the cemetery's viewing room. No doubt the staff had thought they had seen everything—celebrities can have notably eccentric requests, after all—but they were in for a surprise when they opened the shoebox. Certainly, this was the first time anyone had ever brought in a supermarket chicken for burial. Nevertheless, they held their tongues, and perhaps their noses, and gave Blinky the same respect as any other deceased pet. She was laid out in a small coffin so that Vallance could visit her one last time, and then taken away for burial on the grounds.

Skeptics are quick to question the motives behind Blinky's funeral. Some suspect that the episode was an elaborate prank at the expense of the cemetery, or perhaps a misguided piece of performance art intended to mock the genuine sorrow people feel upon the death of a pet. But Vallance has always denied such accusations, insisting that the act of choosing Blinky and then memorializing her created a shared experience that, while short in time, had nonetheless

1976   1978

BLINKY

THE FRIENDLY HEN

JEFFREY VALLANCE

left them linked. And as proof that their bond was more than just a dalliance, he has returned repeatedly to the subject of Blinky, not merely by visiting her grave, but by staging a series of exhibitions based on her postmortem journey. These have featured stand-ins lying in state in a coffin similar to the original, as well as the display of various mementos, including reliquaries containing bones retrieved after a partial exhumation.

Vallance has by now spent more than four decades tending the legacy of his adopted fryer chicken, which is a singular accomplishment in its own right. But has he succeeded in making a point about how society categorizes animals? This is a tricky question to answer. To a small audience, yes, but overall the story tends to leave most people with confusion rather than a moral. And whether Blinky fits best in art history, funerary history, or the history of activism is likewise a matter of debate. However one judges, there is an outcome on which all would agree. As Vallance has explained in interviews, he saved Blinky from her intended fate of being just another anonymous bird to be eaten and forgotten. That much is beyond doubt. Jeffrey Vallance indeed ensured that this particular chicken did not pass from the world unnoticed, and she is remembered still, with "Blinky the Friendly Hen" inscribed upon a gravestone to carry her name forward for posterity.

As for her final resting place, Blinky's presence among some of the world's most renowned pets might at first seem incongruous. But is it not deserved? After all, she has gained her own unique distinction as the world's most famous— indeed, only famous—fryer chicken. Destined from birth for a belly, she was plucked away from a butcher's aisle at the last moment, to make her name in an Elysian field among the high and mighty. In a cemetery where the outlandish has always been commonplace, and where the weirder something is the better, Blinky reigns supreme. The most unlikely celebrity of all, hers is a true Hollywood story if ever there was one.

Relics and the restaging of her funeral have ensured Blinky remains the world's most famous fryer hen.

V

Heroic Animals
The Dogs of War
& A Very
Special Cat

V

 Lost Graves and Stuffed Heroes:
The Fate of Early Combat Dogs

On May 22, 1961, a color guard of United States Marines lifted their rifles skyward over a Southern California pet cemetery and waited for the signal to fire in salute. The grounds before them were barren, save for a single empty grave next to which a coffin lay containing the body of a German shepherd. Sea Breeze Pet Cemetery in Huntington Beach was new, but that was not the sole reason why, up until then, it had been virgin land. Plots had been reserved and could have already been occupied by various local pets that had passed away, but these burials had been willingly delayed when it became known that a very special canine hero would soon pass: Sarge, the last surviving World War II dog. He had been offered a grave as a gift of the new cemetery, and it was decided that, in thanks for his selfless service, his should be the first interment.

That the cemetery itself was to be founded upon Sarge's burial, with a color guard standing alongside his grave, was a dramatic demonstration of the level of respect that canine soldiers engender. Almost every pet cemetery of even moderate size seems to have a military dog buried there, and their graves are invariably among the most esteemed on the grounds. And they are not just found in pet cemeteries. Some are laid to rest with honor on military bases while others have been given memorials in public parks. The respect for them is great enough that some have even been laid to rest in cemeteries intended for humans, and they are the only class of animals that have managed such burials without undue controversy.

Their graves are so ubiquitous that it is hard to believe it was not always this way. Graves for war dogs are in fact a fairly new phenomenon, another invention of the 19th century, but even then they were uncommon, and generally absent from the earliest pet cemeteries. Hyde Park had none, although perhaps to make good one was added later: even though the cemetery had been closed for over half a century, room was found for a Royal Marines commando dog named Prince in 1967. None are recorded among the early interments at Molesworth and Hartsdale either. The Cimetière des Chiens at least had Pompon, who had lived among the soldiers at a nearby military training ground, among its first burials, although he was a mascot rather than an actual combat dog.

Throughout most of history, true war dogs received little recognition. There are legends of some being given memorials in the ancient world, such as a dog named Sorter who was claimed to have saved Corinth by raising the alarm over a surprise invasion of Athenians. It is impossible to confirm such stories, however. Primary sources simply don't substantiate them, and they may have been the romantic inventions of later generations of dog lovers.

It was not until the Renaissance that a canine soldier finally managed to pierce the veil of anonymity and garner widespread acclaim. Becerrillo, a mastiff–greyhound mix serving with the Spanish in the conquest of Puerto Rico, was first mentioned in 1511, and soon became renowned for performing what the Conquistadors referred to as "very wonderful and marvelous feats," which basically amounted to terrorizing uncooperative natives.[1]

The islanders were said to be more afraid of Becerrillo than they were of the Spanish soldiers, and he was rewarded for his efforts with a share of the spoils, slaves to tend his needs, and a cloak that wrapped around his body to protect him from poisoned arrows. His reign of terror lasted only until 1514, however, when he took several poisoned arrows to the ribs, apparently having gone chasing after a group of rebels without wearing his cloak. The great Becerrillo would seem a likely candidate for a grave, or at least some kind of posthumous monument, but even he did not receive one, at least publicly. Whatever the Spanish did with his body was kept secret: since the natives considered him invincible, it was decided it would be best to not do anything that might acknowledge his death.

Not until 1811 is there sufficient testimony to affirm that a war dog was given a grave. This honor went to one of the great names in canine history, Moustache.[2] He was of an entirely different type than his predecessors like Becerrillo, who gained fame for brutality. Fittingly for a century in which animals were being increasingly humanized, Moustache earned distinction for loyalty, bravery, and comradeship. These are the characteristics that would afterward become prized in service dogs. That these are ideal traits for a human soldier as well is perhaps why they finally started receiving graves. With Moustache came a new breed, a type of dog who could be considered as much a soldier as he was an animal.

Born in 1799 in Normandy, Moustache is typically listed as a poodle, although in those days poodles were close in breed to a barbet. His career began with French grenadiers at Marengo, but it was at Austerlitz that his reputation was forever secured. An ensign carrying the regimental colors had been mortally wounded. He was surrounded by the enemy when he expired, leaving the flag free for the taking. None of the French soldiers could have reached it in time—or at least none of the human soldiers. But a dog could.

Engraving after a 19th-century painting of Moustache rescuing a tattered French flag at Austerlitz.

Moustache darted across the battlefield, dodging bodies as they fell around him and deftly weaving through a maelstrom of legs. Using his paws, he pulled the flag free from the dead man and then grabbed it with his mouth.

Moustache had the French flag! He was also himself now encircled, and in the ensuing fracas one of his legs was broken. But he never gave up the flag, scrambling free, making a mad dash for the French lines, and carrying it to safety. There had never been anything like it. This was not the act of a brute animal, and afterward Moustache was officially recognized as a soldier, with his name added to the official regimental ledger and pay and rations issued on his behalf. He was also presented with a medal, hanging from a tricolor collar and inscribed on the front, "Moustache, A French dog, a brave fighter entitled to respect," and on the back, "At the Battle of Austerlitz he had his leg broken while saving the flag of his regiment." And as a final reward, when he returned to Paris he was given an audience with Napoleon, which proved an even greater triumph. Moustache was adept at learning tricks and had been taught to lift his leg and urinate on hearing the names of the emperor's enemies. Napoleon was understandably enraptured.

Not resting on his laurels, Moustache accompanied the French army to Spain, where he was killed by a cannonball at the Siege of Badajoz. To honor a hero's memory, his comrades dug a grave at the spot where he had fallen. He was laid to rest with his medal clasped around his neck, under a stone

A hero finally given his due: Moustache's lost grave was recouped by this cenotaph in Paris.

In this rare World War I photo, a German soldier pulls a dog's body to its grave.

on which was written, "Here lies brave Moustache." It was a historic gesture, courtesy of men who respected him as an equal. Unfortunately, the Spanish were not keen on hosting the burial of a French canine hero, and when they retook Badajoz, Moustache's remains were exhumed, burned, and scattered to the wind.

It was a galling end for one of history's most important animals, but the loss of the grave prophesied what would be a consistent problem for war dogs in the 19th century. Unlike the case of human soldiers, for whom attempts were made to ship the body home or evacuate it to a military cemetery, dogs killed in combat were buried in makeshift graves near where they fell. This created obvious challenges in terms of preservation, since the graves were hastily dug, and either not marked or commemorated only with temporary markers that deteriorated over time until they were lost to history. In Moustache's case, the lost grave was recouped by the placement of a cenotaph at Cimetière des Chiens. It sits by the gate, a small, rough-hewn block of stone on which a metal plate is inscribed with his name and the epitaph, "A Hero of the Grand Army." But it took nearly two centuries for even the most famous military dog in French history to receive his due, the stone not being placed until 2006, and there were precious few others with the kind of cache that would inspire later generations to honor them.

Numerous war dogs were known to have been buried during the American Civil War, for example, and of all of them only one, Sallie Ann Jarrett, now has a memorial of any kind, and it is likewise not at her gravesite. A bulldog–terrier mix who served valiantly for four years with 11th Pennsylvania Infantry, she was remembered in 1890 when her regiment unveiled a monument at Gettysburg.

A soldier with his gun held high stands atop a platform, and at the base rests a life-sized bronze sculpture of Sallie Ann, lying peacefully with her head upon her paws. Her actual grave, however, went unmarked, some two hundred miles away at Hatcher's Run, Virginia, where she was killed by an errant bullet in 1865.

At Edinburgh Castle, meanwhile, a small burial ground, the Cemetery for Soldiers' Dogs, had been founded during the 1840s in a grassy clearing on a parapet.

The little cemetery is often misunderstood, however. It is considered the oldest surviving burial ground dedicated to military dogs, although it is not a graveyard for *war* dogs. The difference is not just semantic: the cemetery in Edinburgh was for pets owned by military personnel, not canines who had served in combat. There are, for instance, dogs buried there who were owned by military marching bands, and of the two dozen weathered headstones still present, there is only one for a dog known to have had a lengthy service record. Dobbler, who died in 1893, spent nine years with the Argyll and Sutherland Highlanders in China, Sri Lanka, and South Africa, although he seems to have been something more like a mascot with a full passport than an actual war dog.

There is, however, a genuine 19th-century canine soldier to be found at Edinburgh Castle, and his presence there helps explain the dearth of gravesites for the combat dogs that returned home alive. This is Bob, and he is not buried in the cemetery, but rather stuffed and on display in the castle's War Museum. He had deserted his former owner, a butcher, to take up with the 1st Battalion of the Scots Fusilier Guards in 1853, and a year later shipped out for the Crimean War.[3] His most remarked upon trait was chasing cannonballs, but foolhardy hobbies aside he wound up serving what turned out to be a historically important role. Bob became the first dog to scour the battlefield for injured men. If they were conscious, he would lick their face to boost their morale and offer brandy from a flask around his neck, and if they

Two 19th-century canine heroes wearing their medals. Bob earned his in the Crimea, while Bobbie made his name in Afghanistan and his medal was presented in an audience with Queen Victoria.

were unresponsive, he would bark out a distress call to alert medics. By World War I, the Red Cross was training dogs to find men just as he had, making Bob a pioneer and justly earning him the medal that he still wears today.

While pet owners mostly shied away from taxidermy, soldiers considered it preferable for animals like Bob. The thought at the time was that, compared to burial, taxidermy was a better way to perpetuate the legacies of these historically important dogs, since they could then be displayed in regimental museums for visitors to see. This was especially true in Britain, where there was something of a fad for it, and among those still preserved is the most famous of all, a mutt named Bobbie from the 66th Berkshire Regiment.[4] Eleven men were left trapped among the enemy when British forces withdrew at the Battle of Maiwand in Afghanistan in 1880, with Bobbie among them. Yet he did not flee, choosing to stand firm at their side, barking and biting at all-comers. He received a deep slash along his back from a scimitar in the ensuing fight, and after his comrades were all felled he made his way to safety, walking forty-five miles alone through hostile terrain. The story of his bravery and loyalty made him a legend, something like the English version of Moustache, and earned him a campaign medal presented in an audience with Queen Victoria.

Taxidermy remained a postmortem treatment for famous war dogs through World War I, and among those stuffed was Sergeant Stubby of the American 102nd Infantry. One of the most celebrated dogs of the war, Stubby was credited with capturing a German prisoner, literally catching him by the seat of the pants. He maintained a high profile in retirement as the mascot of Georgetown University in Washington, D.C., and was a much-loved presence around the nation's capital. One of the most enduringly popular of all American war dogs, his legend eventually inspired an animated feature film, released in 2018, and he remains on display at the Smithsonian Institution.[5]

World War I represented a turning point in the postmortem fates of canine heroes, however. Isolated examples like Stubby aside, taxidermy was losing popularity. No doubt this was due to the sheer number of exceptional dogs that served, cumulatively holding a far more important role than a few stuffed specimens on museum shelves could adequately testify to. In previous conflicts, dogs like Moustache or Bobbie, those that could be considered on the level of a soldier, were novelties. But in World War I they were everywhere, with seemingly every battalion able to relate some outstanding story of canine heroism.

This was an unexpected development, since leading into the conflict it was believed there would be no role for animals at all. It was to be the first "modern war," with the technological innovations that preceded it, from airplanes to radios to tanks, expected to make animals an anachronism. Yet animals wound up indispensable as new technologies often proved unreliable, and in the end more dogs took to the field than in any war in history. A modern idea that didn't fail, however, was to give these dogs an increasing variety of duties.

No longer simply serving as sentries or attack dogs, they were pressed into service delivering messages, carrying medical supplies, sniffing out mines or broken communication wires, and performing various other indispensable tasks. Savvy soldiers even learned to rely on their dogs as a form of first alert, since they could more quickly scent out gas attacks, or hear the whiz of a flying shell before it could be registered by the human ear.

Not only did these dogs combine to save countless human lives, some were even credited with influencing the outcome of battles. Of course, more canine combatants in a greater number of roles resulted in yet another new development: more canine casualties than ever before. Battlefield burials were previously limited to single dogs, but so many worthy canine soldiers were killed in World War I that entire makeshift cemeteries began popping up to hold them. Little is recorded of these burial grounds, but photographic evidence testifies to their existence. There is, for example, a photo of a crude German war dog cemetery, the graves marked by white wooden boards, with a soldier pulling a dead dog by its front legs.

These makeshift graves, like those before them, were destined to be lost. A way was needed to prevent a generation of canine heroes from falling into obscurity, and it wasn't just their fellow soldiers who wished for their sacrifice to be honored. Radios, telegraphs, and wire services had allowed the public to follow World War I in a more timely and comprehensive manner than any previous conflict, and dog-loving members of the public had been made well aware of canine heroism. In fact, something of an obsession had grown around

After the war Stubby was a celebrity, here posing with a Washington, D.C., girl during a parade.

dogs from the war, especially in the United States, where their role had been the most underestimated. Of all the major combatants, the Americans were the only ones to enter the war without a dog program, forcing them to borrow dogs from their allies and rely upon strays found along the way.

The stunning success of this ragtag crew made a great impression back home. Like Stubby, many of the dogs who survived attained celebrity status, and were sought out across the country to make appearances at parades and veterans' events. But what of the countless unlikely heroes that had given their all, only to be buried in hastily made graves on distant battlefields? There was a groundswell of sentiment to find a way to do right by them. The task of honoring their sacrifice would fall to that quirky invention that over the preceding two decades had been gaining popularity among animal lovers: the pet cemetery. And within a year of the cessation of hostilities, one of them already had a unique memorial in the works.

The Golden Age: The War Dog Memorial and US Canine Heroes

Most of the canine soldiers that survived World War I had been young during the fighting, so the bulk of them did not pass until the late 1920s. But the reverence for their valor was such that the American public could not wait to memorialize them. Immediately at the war's end, a movement began to honor all the dogs that had served—both the survivors and those that had been killed in action— by creating a new kind of monument. Hartsdale Pet Cemetery heard the call and began soliciting designs and donations, and by 1919 was able to announce that the world's first War Dog Memorial was planned for its grounds.[6]

Work was not completed until 1923, but the wait produced one of the most influential monuments ever dedicated to animals, and certainly the most influential ever constructed in a pet cemetery. If it no longer seems like a revolutionary idea, it is because it has been copied so often as to seem familiar, with its descendants found throughout the world. Some are instantly obvious, looking nearly identical. Others less so, having incorporated human figures to stress the bond between soldiers and their canine comrades, and some have expanded the original theme to include more than just dogs. But when the original was unveiled, a public monument paying homage to animals as military heroes was an entirely novel idea.

The War Dog Memorial was cast in bronze and stressed the role of the dog as an agent of mercy. A German shepherd, donning a Red Cross jersey like those of the dogs that rescued wounded men on the battlefield, stands atop a

DEDICATED
TO THE MEMORY OF
THE WAR DOG
ERECTED BY PUBLIC CONTRIBUTION
BY DOG LOVERS, TO MAN'S MOST
FAITHFUL FRIEND, FOR THE VALIANT
SERVICES RENDERED IN THE
WORLD WAR
1914 — 1918

boulder and stares out over the horizon. At the dog's feet are a canteen and helmet, symbols of the soldiers who owed their lives to the brave canines that came to their aid. Beneath is an inscription reading, "Dedicated to the memory of the war dog. Erected by public contribution by dog lovers, to man's faithful friend, for the valiant services rendered in the World War, 1914–1918."

The importance of the memorial was emphasized by its size and placement: reaching ten feet at its apex, it towers above all the other monuments in the cemetery, and standing along a main pathway it created a focal point for the grounds. It was instantly popular and remains so to this day—the most iconic monument in the one of the world's most famous pet cemeteries. No longer a site that solely commemorates dogs from World War I, the War Dog Memorial now stands in honor of all dogs that served, no matter the conflict, with a ceremony held every Memorial Day to offer a wreath at the bronze dog's feet.

Hartsdale's new creation basked in the glow of what had become a kind of canine golden age in the United States. Inspired by the dogs that had served in the war, the American public became obsessed with canine greatness. From action stars on the silver screen like Rin Tin Tin to touching stories from daily life, dogs and their doings were bigger news in the 1920s than they had ever been before or since. Heroic dogs were such the rage that when a husky named Balto led a sled team that in midwinter 1925 ran a package of serum into Nome, Alaska, during a diphtheria outbreak, he was rewarded with a statue in Central Park. This put him in the company of no less than William Shakespeare and Ludwig van Beethoven.

But of all the great dogs that graced the public stage during this era, none captured the heart of the American public the way a feisty mutt discovered by a group of soldiers in a Paris alley in early 1918 did, and his grave at Aspin Hill remains the most famous of any canine soldier in the United States. A mixed-breed terrier, he was such a mess when he was first found that the soldiers thought he was a pile of rags, so Rags became his name. It wasn't an auspicious beginning, yet this little mess would prove himself many times over.[7]

The initial basis for Rags's fame was his service record, which was exemplary enough that he was named the official mascot of the entire American First Army.

Hartsdale's War Dog Memorial inspired numerous others and remains an important ceremonial site.

The hero of Nome, Alaska, Balto posed for a photo with local twins on arriving in Seattle.

In particular, his ability to run messages through enemy fire saved the lives of many soldiers. This did not make him unique, of course, and his renown after the war, which dwarfed that of the other war dogs, was greatly aided by a pair of extenuating factors. One was location: he spent most of his life at Fort Hamilton in New York City, and this proximity to the media hub of the country ensured his continued presence in the news cycle. The other factor was more personal, having to do with the nature of Rags himself.

Rags was no dashing hero out of central casting, but rather an irredeemably common mongrel whose faults were glaring and eccentricities numerous. His distaste for being bathed and brushed ensured that he never appeared much less of a mess than on the day he had been found. In addition, the war had left him blind in his right eye and missing the tip of an ear and part of a paw. And he didn't exactly bear his afflictions with dignity, being frequently gruff, with little patience for the demands his own celebrity had brought. Yet no more loyal dog could ever be found. He was, in short, the quintessential lovable lout—and this made him utterly irresistible.

It also resulted in social connections that were impressive by any standards, and for a half-blind mongrel with tangled hair seemingly inconceivable. Rags might be found in the company of New York's most eligible young ladies as a guest at debutante balls, for example, or at luxury hotels making appearances at charity events. At army functions he was a bigger draw than any general. But through it all he was always Rags, so hopelessly out of place in high society that he once slid across a tiled floor at a Park Avenue soiree and knocked over all the teacups. On another occasion, he kept a contingent of high-ranking British and American officers waiting at a book signing for his own biography. It had been published in 1930, and the Imperial War Museum had requested a pawtographed copy. Rags had been asleep on a coal pile the day of the event, and the VIP audience and media corps were treated to the

Rags's fame after World War I made him as big a name as any army general.

ungainly sight of their guest of honor trailing a cloud of black soot all the way to the podium.

Such stories made everyone love Rags all the more. Everyone, that is, except breeders of expensive purebred dogs, for whom the rancorous terrier loomed like Darth Vader. In fact, they had good reason to fear him. In 1925, Rags's soldier buddies decided he should be part of the prestigious Long Island Kennel Club Show. That an ill-tempered mutt was denied entry into a show of purebreds is no surprise, but the backlash that ensued was unprecedented. Pardon our "son of battle on four legs," but he must have left his pedigree behind "at the front—along with that eye and ear that he lost saving the lives of American boys," railed one editorialist. The same writer continued by insulting the club's dogs as "the canine counterpart of lounge lizards."[8] Beaten into submission by vitriol, the Kennel Club eventually invited Rags to be their guest of honor. He was seated at the entrance to the show, contentedly eating dog biscuits and leaving a terrible mess of crumbs on the floor, while the Kennel Club swept up after him, not daring to offer a word of complaint.

In contrast to such hoopla, Rags's death came quietly. In 1934, he had moved to Washington, D.C., with the family of his caretaker, Lt. Colonel Raymond Hardenbergh, and would spend his final two years there. His passing was reported on March 22, 1936, with the obituary running as a lead story throughout the country. Considerable debate followed as to how America's most beloved canine hero should be memorialized. Grand ideas were bandied about, and the general assumption was that he would be returned to New York for burial. The discussion was moot, however. Rags had in fact died over two weeks prior, on March 6, and had been secretly buried at Aspin Hill. Not even the army had been informed.

The secrecy was intended to avoid undue commotion, and was typical of the quietude that surrounded the final years of the dog's life. By that time, Rags was old and sickly, and had been kept out of the public eye by Hardenbergh in order to spare his admirers the pains of a hero laid low by the ravages of time. Aspin Hill included boarding and medical facilities, and Rags had been placed there to receive special care. Hardenbergh and Aspin Hill's owner, Richard Birney, had interred him in the cemetery's grounds just a short walk from where he had passed.

As it turned out, however, Rags couldn't leave without creating a final ruckus. His grave was initially marked only by an American flag, making him one of the first war dogs to receive what is now a common honor. When a visitor to the cemetery publicly questioned the appropriateness of placing the nation's flag at the grave of a dog, Rags's friends and fans answered in emphatic terms, dotting the ground all around his grave with flags, and thereby providing a fitting end for a stray from the alleys of Paris who had turned himself into an American icon.

Rags's death was the end of an era, but World War II and the wars that came after created new generations of canine heroes, with hundreds more unique

graveside stories. The most unlikely involved history's smallest war dog, Smoky. One of the greatest mysteries of World War II was how a stray, four-pound Yorkshire terrier wound up in the middle of a combat zone in the New Guinea jungle. The soldier who found her was a bad enough poker player that, to cover his stake, he sold the little stranger for two dollars to Corporal Bill Wynne of the 26th American Photographic Reconnaissance Squadron, and under his tutelage she became one of the most notable dogs of the war.[9]

As an unparalleled morale booster, the mighty mite was famed for performing tricks in military hospitals, where her mere presence proved a better medicine than anything the physicians could prescribe. But her wartime service was not all a show: when Smoky was most needed, during the invasion of the Philippines, she delivered. A runway was scheduled to be torn up in order to lay communications wires, and this would have grounded American planes and invited an enemy attack. But there was an alternative. A pipe eight inches in diameter ran the length of the runway, and there was one soldier just small enough to pull a wire through—to a rousing ovation when she made it out the other side.

Smoky lived out her life after the war with Wynne in Ohio, dying in 1957. She was buried at the Cleveland Metroparks Rocky River Reservation, in a grave initially marked only with stones. But thanks to a $30,000 fundraising campaign, a permanent marker was finally placed over the spot on Veterans Day, 2005.

Nearly a century after his death, Rags's grave is still the most famous burial at Aspin Hill.

Smoky's grave marker is based on a photo by her owner of the dog in an army helmet.

A suitably adorable memorial for history's most adorable soldier, Smoky is depicted in bronze sitting inside an army helmet, with an inscription that declares her a "Yorkie Doodle Dandy."

But for the most dramatic burial ever given a combat dog, none can compare to that Southern California spring day in 1961, with the Marines Corps color guard pointing their rifles to the sky over what was about to become Sea Breeze Pet Cemetery. Like Smoky, Sarge served in the Pacific Theater during World War II. But whereas the war seemed to be a succession of smiling faces for the charismatic little dog, for Sarge it was blood and guts.[10] He had been adopted in 1941 at the age of six months by Army Sergeant Edward Platt as a gift for his wife, Jeanne. The dog did not get much time with his new family, however, since the Platts felt it was their patriotic duty to offer him for military service after the United States entered the war later that year.

Sarge was assigned to the Marine Corps and became a Devil Dog. This was the name for the dogs who served in battle on remote tropical islands, and they are perhaps history's most legendary combat canines. In extreme humidity and dense jungle, they faced harsher conditions than any other war dogs have ever endured, yet they saved countless lives with their ability to warn of ambushes, scent snipers, and detect mines. They also suffered high casualty rates, being frequently targeted by the enemy, who was well aware of their effectiveness. They were esteemed enough that a special cemetery was built in 1944 at Asan, Guam, to honor those killed in combat. And their legacy continued to be revered, with a new cemetery built after the original was destroyed by a typhoon in 1963. This one was then restored and rededicated in 1994, with a life-sized bronze statue of Kurt, the first of the Devil Dogs to die in action, added as a centerpiece.

Sarge was among those who made it back alive, although it was no easy path, taking him through such major centers of battle as Guadalcanal, Tarawa, and Saipan. The Marines had a system for ranking dogs, all of them starting as a private but able to rise as high as sergeant based on meritorious service. "Sarge" was merely a nickname he picked up as he rose through the ranks,

Sarge waiting backstage before making a public appearance during Los Angeles Animal Week in 1956.

with his proper name, as given to him by the Platts, being Major Von Luckner, after the Luckner kennel where he was bred. This made him the only member of the United States military who could go from major to sergeant and consider it a promotion, with his stripes earned by dragging nine wounded soldiers from the battlefield to safety.

It was during the ninth rescue that Sarge nearly lost his life, taking a bullet to the head while pulling an injured Marine out of the line of fire. When medics arrived, they began tending the human soldier, but showed no inclination to do the same for the canine one, who was lying nearby. But the dog had risked his life for a comrade, and the favor was now returned. The wounded Marine adamantly refused any assistance unless it was offered equally to Sarge, which is how he wound up at a mobile hospital. A surgeon there improvised as best he could, cutting a metal plate from a mess kit and inserting it under his scalp.

Sarge was rewarded with a Purple Heart. Added to his nine other citations, including a Silver Star for heroism under fire, he is one of history's most decorated war dogs, although he most likely cared more about going home than he did about the medals. But once back stateside, he again faced death. Exactly how Sarge wound up sickly and starving in a Los Angeles tenement remains unknown. The Marines had what seemed like a failsafe system for detraining and returning service animals, but in his case the process was somehow botched, and he

While the gravestone at Sea Breeze Pet Cemetery lists him as Major Von Luckner, the public knew him as Old Sarge, and that name graces his statue on the walkway leading into the grounds.

wound up abandoned. Taken in by a dog catcher, he likely would have been put down were it not for a technician at the city pound. The man had been a battlefield medic, and when he stroked the poor dog and felt the metal plate under his scalp, he knew this was no ordinary stray.

When Sarge's identity was finally confirmed, he was sent back to Jeanne Platt, although death would never stop stalking him. At one point, when he was fourteen, illness dropped his weight to a mere thirty pounds, and no one had any doubt that the reaper would soon come calling. Yet Sarge once again proved too tough a foe, rebounding to outlive every other dog that had served in the war. Not that anyone was counting the years at first. It was when he turned sixteen that people began to take notice. That's when he became Old Sarge, the nickname by which he became best known.

A party was arranged for his seventeenth birthday, and the newspapers wrote about the incredible saga of the old war dog, the last of the line. There was a sentimental air to the story since those on hand believed it would be the last chance to tell it. But Sarge was not quite done outrunning death. His eighteenth and nineteenth birthdays were celebrated with increasing pomp. One more would make twenty, an unfathomable age even for a German shepherd that had never taken a bullet to the head.

All wondered if there was any chance this canine Methuselah could make it that far, and more than a hundred guests were on hand to celebrate when he did. It was the feel-good national news story of the day—the tough old soldier dog who had made cheating death his life's work. Privately, though, those close to Sarge knew there would be no more birthdays. With the end of his journey in sight, ideas were discussed for a way to honor him that would remind the public not only of his sacrifice, but of the many others like him. That is when the new pet cemetery stepped in and offered their first grave, and in addition something more: a statue to be placed at the entrance, yet another war dog memorial, but bearing Sarge's name, as a place where people could leave flowers and offerings.

None too soon was the decision reached, as on May 17, 1961, a month and a day after Sarge's final birthday party, death finally caught its elusive prey. Five days later, after a telegram from the governor of California was read at his graveside, the color guard lifted their rifles. A final gift was then placed alongside his body, a briar pipe that had belonged to his last Marine handler, and his casket was lowered into the ground as the order was given to fire. With the echoing of the guns, word was carried on the wind that a new *terra sancta* for pets had been consecrated, in memory of one of the greatest animal heroes. It was a fitting gesture to be sure, and the cemetery has continued to esteem Sarge ever since, with Memorial Day celebrations at his statue and his medals displayed in the office. But even with such honors, when it comes to paying tribute to heroic animals, there is one burial ground in England that stands above all others.

Where Legends Lie:
The PDSA Pet Cemetery in Ilford

The most hallowed of animal burial grounds hardly seems so special at first. Quiet, curving streets lead past drab block houses, and upon arrival the would-be pilgrim is confronted not by the gates of paradise, but by a plain brick building that houses the Ilford branch of the People's Dispensary for Sick Animals. Yes, there is a pet cemetery around back, but it is likewise unremarkable at first glance: the grounds are small, the landscaping seems an afterthought, and only a scant few of the graves are impressive to behold. It is only when one reads the names inscribed on the headstones that an impression is finally made, and for those who recognize them it can be a humbling experience. In no other pet cemetery is there a greater concentration of heroic animals. And not just any heroic animals, these are the most holy of the holies. This place is, in effect, the animal world's version of Valhalla.

That these graves are here is thanks to the vision of Maria Dickin. Born the daughter of a minister in London in 1870, she became involved in social work in the city's impoverished East End, and the privation she found there changed the course of her life. It was not the conditions under which the human residents were living that moved her, however, but rather how their destitution affected local animals. She had grown up sheltered from the reality of dogs and cats raw with mange and dragging broken limbs, of sickly goats and rabbits rotting away while still alive, of horses and donkeys left crippled from carrying heavy loads. Their suffering was a revelation, and she vowed that her life's mission would be to alleviate their misery.

In 1917, Maria succeeded in opening the first PDSA to provide free veterinary care to poor neighborhoods.[II] Her zeal was such that more clinics soon followed, and even horse-drawn veterinary wagons to reach remote areas. And in the 1920s, she opened another kind of facility: in a grassy plot behind the Ilford clinic, she established a cemetery to provide honorable burials for pets from poor households. Some traces of the cemetery's humble beginnings are still found, such as a much-weathered, hand-painted wooden grave marker dedicated to "The strays and all ill-treated creatures." As the only operational pet cemetery in London, however, it would slowly change, with more impressive monuments than the poor could afford eventually appearing.

The largest cat's grave in the United Kingdom is here, for example. Made entirely of Sicilian marble, it is the resting place of Mr. Tibb, owned by a wealthy benefactor who had donated a mobile dispensary truck to the PDSA. Some of London's most notable pets also found their way in, such as Peter, a former Chief Mouser to the Cabinet Office. The quirkiest of all British traditions involving

animals, the Chief Mouser is the official cat of the Prime Minister's Office. Peter assumed the title in 1947 and became a public sensation after appearing on the *BBC Tonight* television program.[12] His distinguished career spanned five prime ministers, and was marred by only one blemish—a literal blemish, when he defecated on a doormat only moments before a visit from the queen.

Of course, a few impressive graves and a quirk of British history do not create Valhalla. Ilford's reputation as "England's cemetery for heroic animals" is the result of two more decisions made by Maria Dickin. During World War II, she opened the grounds to pets either owned by the armed forces or which had served roles in civil defense. Soon after, she decided to create a new kind of medal. The latter decision was due to controversies that had resulted from awarding medals meant for human soldiers to animals. We have of course already met several animals that received medals, and many people felt that if they served valiantly they deserved equal honors. But there was also a vocal contingent that believed the practice mocked the sacrifice of human soldiers, and for this reason medals were rarely given to animals before World War II. To be awarded, they had to be earned beyond any shadow of a doubt; even then, however, zealots might still complain.

To ensure that soldiers of fur and feather get their due, the Dickin Medal was created in 1943 as the animal equivalent to the Victoria Cross, the highest medal offered by the British armed forces. It is inscribed on the front with "For Gallantry, We Also Serve," and hangs from a ribbon of green, brown, and pale blue, to symbolize valor on sea, land, and sky. It is the greatest military

The cemetery in Ilford is famous for military graves, but also includes humble and ornate public burials.

A PDSA cat in silent vigil at the coffin of Peter, the UK's Chief Mouser, in 1964.

award an animal can receive, and is offered only to those that have performed some extraordinary service. In the eighty years since its introduction, only seventy-five have been given out, and among those recipients, a dozen were buried in Ilford, the largest collection of them in any single place in the world.[13] Of course, twelve out of seventy-five means that considerably more Dickin Medal winners aren't buried there than are, and the others have wound up in a variety of places, ranging from simple backyard interments within England to as far away as Tanzania.

The fame of the little cemetery in Ilford is therefore based not solely on the number of medal winners, but also on who those twelve are. All of them are among the greatest animal heroes in history. Take, for example, the first to be buried there. Rip was a starving terrier discovered by Edward King in a London bomb shelter in 1940. Not wanting to turn the poor dog out, King adopted him. At the time, King was working as an air-raid warden, and he began taking the dog along as he searched bombed-out buildings for survivors. Rip had not been trained to locate people trapped in rubble. At that point in history no dog had. But his finely tuned canine senses made him far more adept at the task than any human, and during his wartime service Rip was credited with saving over a hundred lives, an extraordinary achievement. The debt owed to him is even greater, however. His example spurred the idea of training dogs to do what he had been doing innately, and an entire new field was born. As the pioneering search-and-rescue dog, Rip is certainly among history's most influential canines.

Many of the most renowned rescue dogs that followed in Rip's paw prints, all legends in their own right, are also buried at Ilford. All served during World War II, and among them is Peter,
a collie who discovered six people at the site of a single bombing in London in 1945. Irma is here as well. She would offer different types of barks depending on the victim's condition, and became the first dog to develop a system to communicate whether she had found a live or dead person. The bravest of all is likewise here, Valiant Rex, who gained fame for searching the most treacherous sections of collapsed buildings. Beauty, the dearest to the PDSA's heart, is also buried at Ilford.

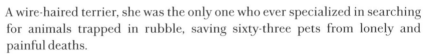

A wire-haired terrier, she was the only one who ever specialized in searching for animals trapped in rubble, saving sixty-three pets from lonely and painful deaths.

There are of course combat dogs as well. In 1940, British soldiers from the King's Royal Rifle Corps in Egypt traded a cup of tea to a local man for a malnourished black mutt. The British soldiers got the better end of the deal. Tich, as they named her, proved to be the outstanding dog of the campaign against the German Afrika Corps, leading medics to wounded men under fire on the battlefield, and even pitching in to dig ditches with her paws. There is also the grave of Punch, a boxer, who along with his sister Judy saved the lives of two British officers from a terrorist's machine gun in Jerusalem in 1946. The dogs sensed the assassin as he laid in wait on a hot summer's night, and as the man prepared to fire, Punch charged forward. He took four bullets, including two to the throat, but survived the attack to live until 1954.

Even among the greats, however, some stand higher. The most legendary dog buried at Ilford is Antis, an Alsatian owned by Jan Bozdech, a Czech airman

Punch's medal was awarded after he survived four bullets that had been intended for British officers.

Rex continued his service after World War II, helping discover victims trapped in a collapsed coal mine.

who flew with the Allies in World War II.[14] Theirs is one of the most remarkable stories in canine history: never have a dog and human together overcome so many obstacles that could have easily ended in tragedy for one or both of them. Even their first day together was the product of a fight for survival. Flying for France after his country had fallen to the Nazis, Jan's plane was shot down and he took refuge in an abandoned barn as he was making his way back to the French lines. That is where he discovered Antis, an abandoned puppy, alone and hungry.

When France fell, he and Antis were captured and placed on a transport ship headed for Italy. It was torpedoed, but they again survived, rescued by the British. Jan was assigned to the Royal Air Force. They knew they were getting a skilled airman in the deal, but could never have guessed what they were getting with his dog. It wasn't long before they got an idea: soon after the pair arrived in the UK, during a bombing raid on Liverpool, Antis ran straight to a pile of wreckage and began to paw furiously. A search team followed and discovered a woman, still alive. He then ran into a dangerous part of the same building and began to bark, calling out for rescuers to help a woman and child trapped there.

It was an incredible performance for a dog with no training, yet is only a footnote to his career. Instead of continuing as a rescue dog, Antis found himself an aviator after he snuck aboard his master's bomber, preparing for a run over Bremen. He kept himself concealed until the plane was in jeopardy. Ice had formed on the wings, an electrical storm had knocked out all communications, the crew was struggling for control of their craft, then suddenly there he was— the surreal touch of a dog mysteriously appearing onboard. When against all odds they made it home safely, the crew decided that perhaps Antis was a lucky charm and invited him to join them full time. He turned out to be more than just a flying mascot: often able to detect enemy aircraft before the plane's radar, he became an invaluable early warning system. And like his crewmates, he faced the dangers of aerial warfare. On one occasion, he was hit in the face by shrapnel. On another, he was lacerated in the belly, losing so much blood he barely survived the flight back.

Even all of that was still only a preface to the service he provided when he was most needed. After the armistice in 1945, Jan returned with Antis to Czechoslovakia, but the peace there did not last. Three years later, a communist coup toppled the government and Jan, having fought for the British, was on a hit list of people who might oppose the new rulers. He and Antis were on the run, setting out with two other refugees, hoping to sneak through the forest to West Germany before they were apprehended. Traveling in the dead of night, the lives of all three men were at the mercy of Antis, who guided them in the darkness past armed patrols and security checkpoints. As they finally neared the border, Antis suddenly disappeared—there was a commotion and Jan ran towards the noise to see that his dog had jumped a guard and pinned him to the ground, thus disabling their last obstacle to freedom.

Returning to Britain in 1949, Antis was awarded a much-deserved Dickin Medal, and dog and master found peace for the next three years. By then he was thirteen years old, however. He began to show signs of age, and on Christmas Eve, 1952, he collapsed. Veterinarians were able to keep him comfortable through the summer, but his condition continued to deteriorate and in August Jan sent a telegram to the PDSA asking their advice. They told him that a dog so great should not be made to suffer; the last line of their response was only two words, "grave reserved." On August 11, Jan took Antis by train to Ilford, where a PDSA vet administered final rest.

A life of unparalleled service ended the only place it could, in Jan's arms. If no dog had ever given more, it meant that no human had ever lost as much, and for Jan there was Antis and only Antis, eternally: he refused to ever own another dog, and would not allow his children to own one either. Instead, he would wait and pray for reunion, the inscription on Antis's gravestone reading, "There is an old belief / That on some solemn shore / Beyond the sphere of grief / Dear friends shall meet once more."[15] Below that, in Jan's native Czech, are the words, "Věrný Až Do Smrti," meaning "Faithful unto Death."

But even Antis, with all the emotion his story provokes, is not the main attraction of the cemetery grounds. That honor goes to Simon, the only cat to have ever received a

Two photos of Antis, plus his grave (overleaf). His paw is held by Field Marshal Wavell's granddaughter at his medal ceremony. The girl presented him an award more to his tastes: a dog biscuit.

Dickin Medal, although his status as the cemetery's star is no mere novelty.[16] He was another of those animals that would have hardly seemed destined for greatness when he was discovered, by British sailors from the gunboat HMS *Amethyst*. They found him in Hong Kong in 1948, a scrawny cat just out of adolescence, stray but friendly. His new friends smuggled him aboard their ship, where he quickly became a favorite of the crew. Having the cat aboard wasn't exactly regulation, but the captain, Lt. Commander Bernard Skinner, decided he could stay. In retrospect, it was a crucial decision.

In 1949, during the communist takeover of China, the *Amethyst* was ordered up the Yangtze River to evacuate the British embassy in Nanking. One hundred miles into its journey, the ship was targeted by enemy gun batteries, with the ensuing salvoes causing it to run aground. Among those killed was Skinner himself, and the *Amethyst* found itself stranded behind enemy lines, its crew effectively held hostage as any attempt at intervention on their behalf might have provoked an international incident. And matters would soon get worse: the *Amethyst* was overrun by rats, preying on the limited rations in the hold.

Simon had taken shrapnel during the attack, yet he nevertheless answered the call of duty. A new battle now unfolded below deck, one in which he would take no prisoners. The war for the ship's rations was important enough on its own terms, but it became something bigger as every rat Simon caught became a cause for celebration among the crew, who kept a running tally. For the suffering sailors,

ANTIS D.M.
ALSATIAN

DIED 11TH AUGUST 1953.
AGED 14 YEARS.

THERE IS AN OLD BELIEF
THAT ON SOME SOLEMN SHORE,
BEYOND THE SPHERE OF GRIEF,
DEAR FRIENDS SHALL MEET ONCE MORE.

VERNÝ AŽ DO SMRTI

incapable of fighting on their own behalf, Simon's victories took on the aura of a battle of hope against despair. And Simon, possessed of the intuition that is typical of the finest animal companions, sensed the effect he was having on the morale of his shipmates. He began tending to their emotional needs, visiting each of them daily and offering whatever form of affection they might accept, even if it was only a nuzzle or purr.

The *Amethyst* was ultimately trapped for 101 days. When the crew finally righted their vessel and sailed free, news spread to the outside world of the role of the ship's cat in their survival. A mania ensued. At every port where the *Amethyst* stopped en route to Britain, there were mail bags filled with cat treats and toys, gifts of his admirers. His volume of correspondence was so great that the Royal Navy had to assign a press officer on his behalf. He was even given his own rank, Able Sea Cat. Simon had become the first international feline celebrity. It was like a fairytale come true—and one that came to a tragic end in Plymouth.

For his human crewmates, the return home meant freedom. But for Simon it meant incarceration, as British bureaucracy demanded he undergo a lengthy quarantine. His death came on November 28, 1949. The hero of the *Amethyst* had survived less than a month in British care, all of it in quarantine, not even long enough to accept his Dickin Medal, which was instead presented posthumously to the ship's new commander, Lt. Geoffrey Weston, nearly five months after his passing. While his death was officially blamed on his wounds, there were more than a few whispers of perhaps a different malady. Simon had, after all, lost his ship, his friends, and his liberty. Had he in truth died of a broken spirit?[17]

Simon's body was sent to Ilford, his residence in Britain having turned out to be nothing more than a grave. If the story was not heartbreaking enough, his burial on December 1 was hastily arranged with only three people present, none of them having known him in life: Grace Macrow, the superintendent of the cemetery, and two gravediggers.[18] It was an unfathomable end, and the public would soon respond with attempts to provide proper memorials. It was at the grave itself that a statement was finally made in the clearest terms about Simon's role as a hero. His current stone grave marker is not, in fact, the original. It replaced one that had deteriorated, since it was made of wood. But not just any wood: this was wood that had been taken from the deck of the *Amethyst* itself. Simon was the heart of the ship, and he was rightly buried under a piece of it.

It wasn't long before Simon became the star of the cemetery grounds. Like an explosion in a florist's shop, his grave was deluged by adoring fans with bouquets and wreaths. It has remained the prime attraction to the current day, enough so that a laminated copy of his thirty-two-page biography is preserved on-site for modern visitors to peruse. Singling Simon out in this way may seem unfair to the other animals. After all, they each gave what they could for causes not of their choosing. But the effect of their graves is not so equal, and Simon's grave justly deserves its exalted standing due to its unique place in history.

We have already noted the long-standing negative stereotypes surrounding felines, and even in Simon's day cats were still a poor cousin to dogs. To the cat-loving public, he represented a crucial figure. More than a naval hero, Simon was in effect a kind of great equalizer, who proved before the eyes of a world that had for so long doubted his species that a cat can indeed possess the same qualities of loyalty and love as the finest canine. As for his death, it cast him in the role of a martyr, and served as a kind of apotheosis through which the image of a feline icon finally put an end to the days of "only a cat."

Imbued with this cultural value, Simon's grave stood not as a memorial to a single cat, but as a kind of altar to feline virtue, and it is a value that it still holds for many people. We can and should judge all the medal winners buried near him, and indeed all those mentioned in this chapter, to be equally heroic. But if we measure the impact of their graves on the world around them, at Simon's we have come to the most hallowed patch of hallowed ground: it is perhaps the most important grave in any pet cemetery in the world.

A sailor among his shipmates, Simon is pictured with crew members of the Amethyst.

OVERLEAF: *Cemetery superintendent Grace Macrow places flowers at Simon's grave, plus his current marker.*

IN
HONOURED
MEMORY
of
"SIMON" D.M.

H.M.S.
AMETHYST.

DIED
NOVEMBER 28TH
1949.

(M 201)

VI

Special Cases

A Sampling of
Unique Burials

VI

Animals have been memorialized in a staggering variety of forms, and there are some surprising posthumous displays. Not all of them are intentional, such as the case of an Alabama dog from the early 20th century who brought on his own demise but in the process gained lasting fame. He climbed into the hollow of a tree, squirmed up far enough to get stuck, and died. Decades later, he was discovered mummified by loggers cutting the tree into sections. While no one has a clue who the dog was during his lifetime, "Stuckie," as he has come to be known, is now displayed within his claustrophobic grave as the main attraction of the Southern Forest World Museum in Georgia. Being interred inside a tree was of course entirely Stuckie's own doing; but in many cases, humans have made decisions in commemorating animals that have resulted in grave sites that cannot easily be categorized. What follow are some favorites.

Rip:
 ## A Deep Sleep

It might be the strangest of all stories surrounding an animal's grave, although rightfully it should be considered two graves. The first came in 1897, when a horned frog was entombed in the Texas town of Eastland. A new courthouse was being built, and in order to test a theory that horned frogs are capable of hibernating for extensive periods of time, one was sealed in a pocket within a cornerstone of the building. We must acknowledge that imprisoning the poor creature was a blatantly cruel act, but rather than spelling the animal's doom it turned out to be merely the start of an unequivocally bizarre new life.

Even the species itself needs an explanation, since to most people it is wholly foreign. The horned frog is not a frog. It is also known as a horned toad, although it is not one of those either. Sometimes it is called a horned lizard, which is closer to the truth since it is a reptile, found in the American Southwest. They are small, round-bellied creatures, around five inches long, and their bodies are covered with tiny spikes that crest around the head. These prehistoric-looking mini monsters possess some impressive abilities. They can, for instance, shoot streams of blood from their eyes at potential attackers up to five feet away.

But can they survive thirty-one years entombed in a courthouse wall? That was the question on February 14, 1928, when the cornerstone was broken open and a motionless horned frog was handed over to a local judge. He held it up as all around looked on in anticipation. And then it happened: the body twitched—the horned frog had woken up from a thirty-one-year nap! The town named him Rip, after Rip Van Winkle, and his story garnered no small amount of controversy. Some animal experts believed it was nothing more than a Texas tall tale, while others claimed his lengthy slumber was possible, and noted precedents in the natural world.

The debate was never settled, but there is no arguing that everything that came after was no less improbable. Rip became a celebrity. A smash during an appearance in St. Louis, he drew 40,000 spectators, and then became the only horned frog ever invited to the White House. President Calvin Coolidge, known for his taciturn demeanor, found his match in Rip. When their gazes met, a staring contest ensued—which Coolidge lost, blinking first. He then used his glasses to prod at Rip, who responded with a look of such annoyance that newspapers around the country reported the story under dramatic headlines such as, "Toad Glowers at Coolidge!"[1]

Rip's second life was not long lived. He died for good on January 19, 1929. Embalmed by a local undertaker, he was placed in a custom-made, glass-topped casket, and achieved another first for his species when he was given a public wake. He was then returned to the courthouse and displayed upon a stone dais in the lobby. This time it was no nap, although it turned out that Rip wasn't exactly resting in peace either. His body was stolen in 1961 and a ransom demanded, but the culprits had miscalculated their actions. The frognapping was met with outrage across the state, and the thieves decided it was best to divest themselves of their hostage. An anonymous caller told the sheriff that Rip was hidden in a vacant office, where he was found wrapped in a bag along with a note declaring him "too hot to handle."[2]

Stuckie's mummy is still trapped inside the tree in which it was found by loggers in Alabama.

Crowd gathered at the courthouse as Rip's motionless body is removed from the cornerstone.

But the failed frognapping didn't prevent someone else from trying. Rip went missing again in 1971, and an anonymous letter arrived with a photo of him posed on that day's newspaper as proof of his custody. Once more he was quickly returned—or was he? In 1976, another anonymous letter was received, claiming that he was still in the thief's possession and that the Rip currently displayed in the courthouse was a fake. A reward of $5,000 was offered to anyone who could prove otherwise, and the challenge was backed by another photo, showing what appears to be the same frog, again placed on the current day's newspaper.[3]

A crucial detail about Rip's anatomy must now be mentioned: at some point in the 1950s, he lost a rear foot after being mishandled. This is clear to anyone who sees him in Eastland, as the lower half of his left hind leg is entirely missing. But it is the right foot that is missing in the photos from 1971 and 1976.[4] The immediate assumption is that the Rip shown in the photos was a fraud, and that whoever sent them was so sloppy as to pass off a horned frog with the wrong missing foot. But comparing those photos to the current Rip invites us to look back at older photos, and the situation becomes more complicated than we might have guessed.

There is a single surviving photo of Rip that can be firmly dated from the period between his lost foot and the first frognapping. It dates to 1953 and the original print is in the archives of the University of Texas at Arlington. The image shows Rip in his casket and is clear enough that the inscription on the dais is legible, so we can be assured that the negative was not reversed. This is the original Rip, and it is the right hind foot that is missing. This conforms to the anonymous photos sent in the 1970s, and it means that it is the Rip currently on display in Eastland that is the fraud!

And that is not the only discernable difference. The tail of the original is seen to be broken off at the tip, whereas the current Rip's tail is not. The original's body is visibly desiccated, while the current Rip's body is full and round. The original's forelimbs are both bent back at the shoulder, then forward at the elbow, both pointing outward, whereas the current Rip's left forearm is bent entirely back, in something like a paddling motion. Not only is the current Rip an imposter, he looks nothing like the original.

The original Rip shows key differences with the one now on display (this chapter's cover image).

Returning to the photos sent in the 1970s, the horned frog pictured conforms exactly to the original Rip, with its correct foot missing, the tip of its tail broken off, and the forelimbs in the same posture. The anonymous correspondent sent yet another letter, upping the bid to $10,000 if anyone could prove the claim wrong and show that the Rip on display at the courthouse was original. No one took up the offer. Nor could they have, because it seems that the letter writer was telling the truth, and that the author of the letters either had the real Rip or one that looks far more like the original than the one now on display.

The case of Rip is now shrouded in another mystery. No further communication was ever received, and the original Rip has vanished without a trace. Meanwhile, we are left to ponder who the horned frog in the glass-topped casket at Eastland Courthouse is, and of that there is likewise no clue. The only thing we can be sure of is that, wherever he came from and whoever placed him in the stead of the original, he will continue to lie in state in tribute to the most famous of his kind, one whose story would be scarcely less bizarre even if he hadn't really slept for thirty-one years.

Forever Faithful:
Shep

No one knew where the scruffy-looking dog came from, the one that showed up on an autumn day in 1936 at the Fort Benton, Montana, railroad station. He had walked in of his own accord and sat down as if he were waiting for the incoming train. Looking on expectantly, he scanned the passengers as they disembarked, and then turned and left in dejection. If that weren't odd enough, he did the same thing the next day, the day after, and the day after that. The staff didn't know what to make of it, but they did know that he was getting thinner each time he came. And a watchman had seen the dog walk over a mile to the river just to get water. Whoever he was waiting for, the poor dog shouldn't have to go hungry or thirsty, so they started leaving table scraps and bowls of fresh water for him. And when they realized he had been sleeping under the depot, they gave him a bed by the fireplace since Montana nights can get awfully cold.

They also gave him a name, Shep, since he was mostly shepherd, mixed with a bit of collie.[5] Eventually, a crew member was found who mentioned how the dog had watched while they placed a casket onto an eastbound train. It contained the body of a sheepherder, and apparently the dog had been his. No one knew the man's name, he had been a real loner, and he and the dog were all the other had. After they loaded the casket, the dog tried to board behind it, but the crew pushed him off. He whined piteously as the door slammed shut,

then trotted down the tracks in pursuit as the train departed. And now he was back at the station, waiting on every new train, looking for a master who would never return.

The basic outline of Shep's story isn't unique. It is the story of the mourning dog, the loyal canine that waits pitifully at the last place a human companion

was seen, or withers away at his lost friend's grave. While they have long been a staple of canine lore, such stories became especially prominent in the second half of the 19th century, as a kind of flipside to the love humans were developing for pets. The first generation of pet cemeteries provided a clear public statement that we were capable of mourning animals. But if that love was true, they would mourn us too, and images of grieving animals started to become popular. George Jesse's *History of the British Dog*, for example, included an image of a dog wasting away over a grave. "Where thou diest, will I die" read the caption, to further emphasize the point.[6]

And it wasn't fiction. In Edinburgh, Scotland's most famous Skye terrier, Greyfriars Bobby, created the modern archetype when he mourned his way into history at the grave of John Gray, but there are plenty of other cases. In Luco di Mugello, Italy, Fido used to walk to the bus stop each morning when his master, Carlo Soriani, headed off to a factory, and then meet him when he returned. But this was during World War II, and one day the bombs came and Carlo never again got off the bus. But that didn't stop Fido from waiting for fourteen more years. The most famous of them all, Hachikō, waited nearly ten years for Hidesaburō Ueno, a university professor who had died of a cerebral hemorrhage, to return to Tokyo's Shibuya Station.

If the basic outline of Shep's story isn't unique, the details are, and as for his grave, it is unlike any other. As his vigil was picked up by the newspapers and printed across the country, Shep became the biggest celebrity in the city, if not the whole state. It was still the Depression back then, and maybe that's why; maybe people whose lives had been mercilessly uprooted could better empathize with a dog that refused to forget a man who the rest of humanity had forgotten. Passengers began routing their tickets through Fort Benton just to meet him. And he was always there, waiting on every train that pulled in.

Archival photos show Shep greeting a train and walking away in dejection. He was never comfortable with his fame, his interaction with passengers due solely to his forlorn hope of finding his lost master.

It's easy to misunderstand Shep's story. If Hollywood were to write it—one might imagine it as a Disney movie—everyone would love Shep and he would love them back. He would bound towards each incoming train through a maze of hands that offered pets and scratches, as if all these strangers were his new best friends. But this would be far from the truth. In no measure is Shep's a feel-good story. Rather, it is the tragic tale of a broken-hearted dog. He was not friendly, especially towards strangers. Many well-meaning people had offered him their homes, but he refused all of them. The attention he received only made him nervous, and he tolerated it because there was one thing in the world

he wanted, the station had taken it away and he prayed that the station would return it. That hope kept him waiting and watching every day for nearly six years. But on each of those days, with every train that came, his heart broke anew.

Shep's vigil ended on January 12, 1942. He was by then old and deaf, and didn't hear the 235 as it barreled around the bend. Eventually he sensed the vibration of the tracks, but he slipped on the icy rails into its path and suddenly it was Fort Benton's turn to mourn. They buried him high on a bluff, with an obelisk placed over the grave. And lest memory fade, they spelled out Shep in big letters and placed a silhouette of him alongside. A spotlight was installed too, so that travelers at night would still have an opportunity to see Fort Benton's famous dog as they pulled into town. And as they looked up at his visage, maybe they would ponder whether somewhere in the Big Sky, as they call it in those parts, where the days are as blue as lapis and the stars shine like crystals, the faithful dog got his reward, finally found his reunion.

Big Man on Campus:
Seal

Mascot animals have a lengthy history. We have already met several that served with military units, but they have found all manner of other homes, from companies to buildings to entire cities. Many of these have received loving memorials, such as a toothless, three-legged stray cat buried in front of the city hall in Natchez, Mississippi, or Morris the Casino Cat, whose ashes are interred under his likeness in a column outside the Gulfport, Florida, casino that was once his stomping ground. Others have received more curious commemorations, most notably Bosco, a Labrador retriever who had been appointed mayor of tiny Sunol, California. His grave is not public—he was buried in the forest in 1994—but he is remembered in the form of a life-sized, faux-fur double in the town's tavern. The tap runs up through his body to his genitals, and if one lifts his left rear leg as a handle, he urinates beer.

But nowhere have mascot animals been as loved, or their memories as esteemed, as on university campuses. This is true especially in the United States, and campuses are dotted with numerous old graves dating to the 1930s and 1940s, a magical period when a quirky crew of stray dogs managed to crash the hallowed halls of academia. Many of the greatest names are still honored, such as Sideways, a Scottish terrier who is buried outside the administration building at Georgia Tech in Atlanta.

Life started tragically for Sideways. She was tossed from the window of a moving car at the age of only seven weeks, but the evil act was witnessed by a group of Tech students, who rescued the poor pup from the street. Her injuries left her with a skewed gait for the rest of her life and inspired her name, but that didn't stop her from claiming the university as her home. In her two and a half short years, she became an indispensable presence at the library, in classrooms, in nearby

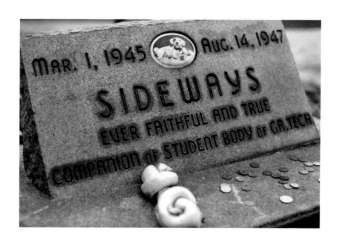

The station has been abandoned but Shep maintains his vigil from his grave on the bluff above.

Sideways still receives tributes atop her campus grave from the students at Georgia Tech.

restaurants, and at campus parties. Her gravestone is still surrounded by an ever-changing display of coins and gifts left by current students, carrying on the tradition of paying homage to their school's favorite canine.

Some of these dogs became such important parts of campus life that they begat proud lineages, including entire burial grounds dedicated to them and their descendants. The University of Georgia, for example, has a mausoleum solely for its mascot dogs, all of them white English bulldogs named Uga, an acronym for the school's name. But none have ever had a funeral quite like the one given to Seal, or "The Great Seal of Virginia," to call him by his full name. He was not the first mascot dog at the University of Virginia. His predecessor, Beta, who is buried near Seal at the university's cemetery, was a hard-living stray who liked to drink beer with the fraternity brothers, which no doubt gained him considerable esteem. Killed by a car in 1939, Beta's funeral is noteworthy in its own right, attracting more than a thousand mourners. But Seal, who showed up as a stray in 1947, would surpass even that. And it was all thanks to an incident on November 5, 1949, that justifiably made him a legend.

Seal had traveled with the school's football team to Philadelphia for a game against the University of Pennsylvania. Penn was a nationally ranked power in those days, and a prohibitive favorite on its home field. The game was tied when Seal took a stroll to the opposing sideline, positioning himself alongside the University of Pennsylvania's cheerleaders. The buzz from the crowd of 78,000 started when he began to lift his leg, some reacting in horror, others in gleeful anticipation. And he did not disappoint, letting loose a stream of urine on the cheerleaders' megaphones. The radio announcers were left with the task of figuring out a polite way to explain to their listeners what all the commotion was about, but the gridiron gladiators from Virginia needed no explanation. Seal had provided his squad with exactly the right motivation,

Statue of Uga I, the University of Georgia's first bulldog mascot, at the mausoleum in Sanford Stadium.

Adjacent to the university cemetery, Seal's grave was the site of the grandest funeral ever given to a dog.

and they pulled away for a twelve-point victory, one that propelled them to the highest ranking to that point in the university's history.

Seal had secured himself a place on the high altar of campus canines, and when he died in 1953, he was treated to a send-off like no other. There are no official records for the size of dog funerals, but Seal's easily ranks among the largest in history. His body was moved in a hearse, followed by the university's band playing Handel's *Death March*, and an estimated two thousand mourners walking solemnly in tow. At the burial site, the captains of twelve university sports teams took their turns as his pallbearers. It was a hero's farewell for a plucky stray who had made himself beloved to a university community and then cemented his status by making the most of his "opportunity with a megaphone," as the athletic department's physician phrased it in his graveside eulogy. Afterward, a large gravestone was placed upon the spot. And lest anyone forget, embedded on the front was a photo that showed Seal wearing a football helmet.[7]

As the football team's twelfth man, Seal made his own winning score from the sidelines.

Mary of Exeter displays her Dickin Medal while in the hands of her owner, Charlie Brewer.

Where Eagles Dare:
Mary of Exeter

Some readers are no doubt already aware of a conspicuous absence in our account of the Dickin Medal winners at the PDSA cemetery in Ilford. All of the heroes there are of course unique in their own way, which is why, singled out for distinction, they were awarded their medals. Yet one of them, Mary of Exeter, truly belongs in her own category.[8] And it is not simply because she is a messenger pigeon who won a medal. That is hardly news, since pigeons are in fact the unsung heroes of the animal world.

If we look at the Dickin Medal as the benchmark of animal heroism, we find that thirty-two of the seventy-five awarded have gone to pigeons. This is well over 40 percent of the total, second only to dogs. If that statistic comes as a surprise, this one will be an outright shock: those thirty-two were among the first forty-five given out, meaning that at one time pigeons owned 70 percent of the most vaunted medals an animal could receive. It is a true testament to their valor, with the proportion having diminished afterward simply because pigeons were eventually taken out of service and therefore had no opportunity to win more.

Stories about these birds nearly defy credibility, such as the heroic flight of the most famous American pigeon of World War I, Cher Ami, who was sent aloft in desperation by the 308th Infantry in the Argonne.[9] Five hundred and fifty-two men were surrounded by the enemy and being pulverized by artillery—their own as it turned out, since the American command was unaware of their position. Human messengers had already been gunned down, and Cher Ami was sent as a last hope, carrying a message with the stranded soldiers' coordinates, and an emphatic plea to stop the barrage.

She was hardly airborne before she was struck in the chest by a piece of shrapnel and plunged to the ground in plain view of the despairing soldiers whose lives depended on her. Yet she wasn't dead. Furiously beating her wings, she rose back into the maelstrom of exploding shells and covered the distance to Signal Corps at nearly sixty miles an hour. She was discovered as a bloody ball of feathers by a sergeant who

hardly knew what he was looking at. There were holes in her chest and wings, and one of her legs had been reduced to mere strands of exposed ligaments. But still dangling from those ligaments, as if by the workings of a parlor magician, was the message capsule.

Cher Ami was nominated for a Distinguished Service Cross and a Croix de Guerre, honors she had certainly earned. But she did not earn a grave. Pigeons simply don't get graves. It's not out of disrespect, it's just not the tradition. Even after taxidermy had gone out of style for war dogs, it remained the choice for avian heroes, Cher Ami among them. But Mary of Exeter was so heroic that she got a grave, the first ever recorded for a pigeon. And that makes her plot very special indeed.

Nicknamed "the bird who would not give up," Mary served with what was called the "Special Section" during World War II, referring to the pigeons that carried messages across the English Channel to and from resistance fighters operating behind German lines. These were the most dangerous flights of all. The overall efficiency of pigeons during the war was rated at 90 percent, yet for the routes Mary flew, scarcely more than 10 percent returned. She survived four of these missions, three under exceptional duress.

On Mary's first flight, she was attacked over Pas-de-Calais by German birds of prey, specially trained to bring messenger pigeons down. She certainly

Mary's grave at Ilford ensures that the valiant service of messenger pigeons is not forgotten.

could not outfight hawks and falcons, and with their talons they ripped a gash from her neck to the middle of her chest. She was presumed dead, yet somehow outmaneuvered her assassins in the skies above the English Channel, arriving four days late and covered in blood. Nursed back to health, she was sent on a second mission and was once again presumed dead. This time she was three weeks delayed, returning with three shotgun pellets in her body and the tip of a wing missing.

The Germans couldn't get her in the air, so they tried on the ground, bombing her loft twice and, in one of the attacks, killing nineteen birds. But not Mary, who survived to again take flight. Exactly what awaited her in the skies on her final mission is unknown, but she did not even have the will to make it all the way home, landing in a field near Exeter with her head lolling alarmingly to one side and bloody cuts traversing the length of her body. She received 22 stitches, the equivalent of 4,000 in a grown man, and the muscles of her neck were so badly damaged that a special collar had to be fashioned to help keep her head upright. But not only did she once again survive, she outlived the war by five years.

Mary's Dickin Medal was presented by Sir James Ross, deputy under-secretary of the Air Ministry, at a ceremony in London on November 29, 1945. When she died in September, 1950, her body was sent to Ilford and given due honors as the first pigeon to receive a public burial. Considering that pigeons had been serving since ancient times, this makes her grave marker something more than a memorial to her alone. The sculpted pigeon between its rails stands as a reminder not just of one bird's heroism, but of the millennia of valiant service from those long-forgotten that have likewise flown their way into animal Valhalla.

 ## *Cruel Ends:*
Stoney, Andy, and Others

Stoney has the distinction of being the largest animal ever buried in a pet cemetery, although it is certainly not an honor that anyone would have wished for an Asian elephant.[10] A fifteen-foot-square by twenty-foot-deep hole was dug for him at Craig Road Pet Cemetery in Las Vegas in 1995, after his death in a storage shed behind the Luxor Hotel. His grave falls into a category that is easy to overlook since it is emotionally the hardest to discuss: memorials for animals that have died from abuse, or were otherwise made to suffer at the hands of humans.

While these graves comprise a very small group, they are nonetheless an important one since they stand as a reminder that cruelty should not be excused by being forgotten. They can have varying purposes. Sometimes they are overtly intended as forms of activism. Aspin Hill has some of this type, products of

a period in the 1980s and 1990s when the cemetery's ownership was under the control of the People for Ethical Treatment of Animals. There is, for example, a grave filled with fur coats, and another for lab rats.

In other cases, they represent collective mourning sites, such as a mass grave at Sunland Pet Rest for 124 greyhounds discovered shot in 1992.[11] In addition, their left ears had been cut off. Locally there was a dog-racing track where the animals were marked with numbers tattooed on the left ear, so it was clear that they were from the track, and their ears had been removed to conceal the identity of the perpetrator. Nevertheless, he was identified: a greyhound racer named Glen McGaughey. According to local statutes, however, it was not technically illegal for him to shoot his own dogs, so he was sentenced to only thirty days of jail time for

Aspin Hill's graves for fur coats and lab rats were lampooned by detractors—the former, for example, was mocked as "The Grave of the Unknown Sable"—but animal activists have always lauded them.

criminal littering. It was an outrageously light sentence in exchange for 124 lives, but a measure of dignity was offered thanks to Sunland Pet Rest's superintendent, who saw to it that the dogs' bodies were interred in concrete vaults at his cemetery, over which a memorial was placed.

Since all graves in this category involve cruel deaths, it is impossible to rate one as more tragic than another, but none are more painful than that of a goose named Andy. Born without feet on a Nebraska farm in 1987, he was acquired by Gene Fleming, who engineered a pair of size-zero high-top baby shoes to fit the stumps of Andy's legs. This allowed him to be fully mobile. No one had ever seen anything like a goose waddling around in sneakers, and he delighted children in particular. He began making the rounds of local schools, but not simply to entertain. Gene intended for Andy to provide inspiration, living proof that no matter what one might suffer and however long the odds, there is no problem that can't be overcome.

It was an irresistible feel-good story. The national media came calling with features in magazines and television shows, and wherever Andy appeared, he brought the same positive message. Despite that, not everyone loved the footless goose. On October 19, 1991, he disappeared from the Flemings' farm. His discovery in a nearby park was a perverse scene, with his head and wings torn from his body. Andy, a symbol of hope whose mission was to bring joy, had been intentionally tortured and killed. His tattered remains were buried on the Flemings' property under a magnificent, oversized granite gravestone, the gift of a local memorial company, which pictured him in his shoes and provided a synopsis of his extraordinary life.[12]

And then there is Stoney, whose story is perhaps the hardest of all to relive. He was owned by a small-time animal trainer named Mike Latorres, who had secured a contract with the Luxor. On September 23, 1994, Stoney was made to practice leg stands when witnesses heard an audible pop. He had torn a tendon in his left hind leg and fell to his knees howling in pain. A veterinarian injected him with morphine and he was moved into a dumpster,

Gene Fleming abandoned his farm, but Andy's grave remains, a symbol of hope extinguished by cruel hands.

which was carried behind the hotel by a forklift. And there, immobilized in a corrugated steel shed, he would spend the next eleven months.

The Luxor had no ownership stake in Stoney, making the injured elephant Latorres's issue to deal with. His care was beyond his owner's means, however, and as time passed, with the Luxor increasingly feeling the ire of animal activists, the hotel's parent corporation eventually put up over $100,000 to tend him. But he fell again in agonizing pain during a therapy session on August 27, 1995. Down for more than twenty-four hours, his body could take no more. He reached his trunk out to Latorres, according to a crane operator on site, but the trainer pushed it away with the admonishment, "Cut it out, Stoney." With his final attempt at human contact rebuffed, the elephant sighed and lost consciousness for the last time.

Latorres at least offered Stoney the dignity of a grave. For many of the activists, this was the closest they had ever gotten to the gentle giant they had hoped to save, and they arrived at his funeral with offerings of peanuts, fresh produce, and signs reading, "We will never forget." And they have not. Even though nearly three decades have passed, fresh flowers and other tokens of affection are still found atop Stoney's headstone. Fortunately, in all those years there has been no need for another hole so large and so deep, and those who work to ensure that animals are treated with due compassion continue the fight in the hopes of keeping this category of grave as small as possible.

The Last Frontier:
Off-the-Grid Pet Cemeteries

They're mostly a desert thing, random groupings of handmade, mismatched memorials rising up against desolate landscapes to proclaim enduring love. But they can be found in any number of other places as well, hidden away in forests or outside remote mountain towns, or anywhere that is similarly possessed of ample public land and a paucity of peering eyes. Makeshift and open to anyone with a shovel, they are usually a locals-only secret. Off-the-grid burial grounds are the last frontier of pet cemeteries, yet they also harkenback to a time long past, being closer in spirit to the renegade burials of the 19th century than they are to any modern, formal pet cemetery.

Offerings are still left at Stoney's grave by those who refuse to let his memory die.

With no one to provide maintenance other than the pet owners themselves, such cemeteries exist in a permanent state of transition, with old burials deteriorating as new ones are added to create an ever-changing visage. This often results in an awkward dichotomy of graves that are lovingly tended sitting alongside those that are abandoned and withering into complete despair. Yet this randomness also makes them the most touching of pet cemeteries. There is no veneer, the graves express grief at its most direct and intimate, and marked with anything from old toys to beer bottles to mailboxes, their lack of pretension and handmade quality make them akin to the *art brut* of mourning.

The greatest concentration of off-the-grid burial grounds is in the American Southwest, where they are descended from their own local traditions rather than the formal pet cemetery network that spread out from the East Coast. In the vast expanses of the desert, rules in the early 20th century were as foreign as snow, so one was free to bury the dead, both human and animal, wherever one chose. Old, handmade graves for dogs in particular are sometimes found near abandoned homesteads and mining camps, and some people took advantage of the lack of governance to be buried alongside their pets.

Eventually, as camps developed into remote towns, the random interments coalesced into small pet cemeteries that became popular burial sites with the first wave of RVers in the mid 20th century. Modern nomads, these road warriors lacked permanent homes, yet needed secure and respectful places to inter animals who had become far more than pets after having traveled sometimes tens of thousands of miles with their human companions. Some off-the-grid cemeteries, such as those in Slab City and Winterhaven, California, are in areas with scant permanent populations and exist solely to cater to pets owned by wanderers.

Not surprisingly, the histories of such cemeteries are difficult to trace. In most cases, only bits of their stories can be retrieved, whatever locals best remember, although it is clear many have historical significance. One of the most prominent, for example, is located in Ajo, Arizona. Its founding is attributed to a man who had been the local de facto veterinarian—he lacked a formal degree and would simply tend animals as best he could—but beyond that little is known. Since no records were ever kept, it is impossible to know when burials started. Several of Ajo's oldest residents say they had interred pets there in the 1960s, however, and one specifically recalls his family burying a dog in 1957, and that there were several graves already present. This would push the first burials back to the early 1950s or perhaps even the late 1940s, making this ad hoc burial ground not only the longest continually active of its kind, but perhaps the oldest pet cemetery in any Southwestern state save for California.

The largest of these cemeteries is in Boulder City, Nevada, and its founding story is similar to that of Ajo's.[13] A man working for the Bureau of Reclamation who once again served as the local de facto veterinarian hatched the idea of a pet cemetery during the mid to late 1950s. It was said the idea was born over drinks, and maybe a lot of them since the original plan had no chance of success: he wanted it incorporated as part of Boulder City's municipal cemetery. When the city declined, he drove out through the desert along Highway 95 and picked out a piece of federal land and began burying pets. Washington, D.C., probably wouldn't have been any more enthusiastic about hosting a pet cemetery than Boulder City was, but the United States government had considerably bigger issues to deal with than a bunch of dogs and cats being buried on an unused and remote parcel of Nevada desert. The cemetery stayed.

One of the reasons for its large size—it spans several acres, and from the highway where very little is visible, the further one wanders, the more graves one finds—is its proximity to Las Vegas. The burial ground in Boulder City is the only one of its kind that is close to a major metropolitan area, and one that had no formal pet cemetery at the time. The desert cemetery was never advertised, and since it was essentially squatting on government land, it technically didn't exist, but word spread and people from Las Vegas began using it as well.

The proximity to Sin City brought something in addition. The Boulder City pet cemetery has developed a notorious reputation, with the legends surrounding it including the mafia using it as a dumping ground for bodies, buried treasure, and any number of claimed ghost sightings. These stories are met with incredulity by locals, but while there may not be any ghosts or mafia victims, there is in fact plenty of buried treasure just off Highway 95. The hot desert sand there is headed into its seventh decade of cradling beloved pets, one of many such no-man's-lands where the last frontier meets the heart.

Handmade graves in Bishop, California, including a mailbox where notes can be left for the deceased dog.

OVERLEAF: *Personal touches found in graves from the Arizona, Nevada, and California deserts.*

BIG   MAMA
REST IN PE CE
990-2009

Rin Tin Tin:
Rin Tin Two?

No other animal has ever ascended to the heights of popularity attained by Rin Tin Tin. As Warner Brothers' most prized golden-age film star, the German shepherd was known as the "mortgage lifter" for his ability to bail the studio out of financial peril.[14] According to a persistent Hollywood rumor, it was he who won the first Oscar for best actor—but was denied the honor when the Motion Picture Academy, worried its award might not be taken seriously by posterity if the initial trophy was given to an animal, ignored the count and gave the statue to his human runner-up. He is still, almost a century after his death, recognized as history's most famous dog.

Given his stature, it is no surprise that his grave, at the Cimetière des Chiens, has become a pilgrimage site. Mentioned on countless websites and included in Paris guidebooks, it draws movie fans from around the world, who leave offerings of flowers and other trinkets. That Rin Tin Tin is buried in France is thanks to his own heritage. He was born in a village in Meurthe-et-Moselle during World War I, the pup of a German war dog, and had been left behind when retreating troops abandoned his kennel. He was discovered by an American GI, Lee Duncan, who smuggled him back to the United States, where he became a legend. After his death, according to the commonly told story, Duncan returned the dog's body to France as an ode to his patrimony. There is a problem with the grave in Paris, however. Rin Tin Tin is not in it: the flowers and trinkets are being left for the wrong dog.

Some backstory is definitely in order. Rin Tin Tin died at Duncan's Beverly Hills home in 1932. A funeral was held in the backyard, where he was buried with his favorite squeaky toy in a bronze casket. There is reliable testimony regarding the grave site, which was under a white rosebush and marked with a cross bearing his name.[15] To get to the Cimetière des Chiens, therefore, Rin Tin Tin would have had to be exhumed and shipped. The oldest surviving notice that mentions a grave for him in Paris is dated 1948, so the transfer would have occurred during the intervening sixteen years.[16] According to most accounts, it was soon after his passing since Duncan had suffered a series of financial setbacks and the house was sold in foreclosure within the year. Yet not a single record exists to indicate that the dog's body was ever sent.

The reason for the lack of records is that it never happened. Duncan's daughter confirms this, saying that she has no knowledge of such an event. Even the cemetery staff, when asked directly, admit they are aware that Rin Tin Tin is not there.[17] So why would anyone think Hollywood's favorite canine star is buried in Paris in the first place? And if he's not in the grave bearing his

name, who is? The answer to both questions, and the reason for the subsequent confusion, is that the grave is not occupied by Rin Tin Tin—but instead contains the body of Rin Tin Tin.

In the late 1930s, a French actor named Teddy Michaud trained a German shepherd for the screen, and by the early 1940s was hiring him out for films. This dog's name was . . . Rin Tin Tin. If it sounds scurrilous to call his movie dog by the same name as the most famous of all movie dogs, Michaud could have rightly claimed that the name was not unique. Duncan had in fact taken the name from Rintintin, a popular French doll. Even so, Michaud's intentions can be nothing but suspect considering the biography he offered, claiming his dog was the son of the original Rin Tin Tin (presumably giving him a birthright to the name), mated with a Brazilian wolf. The story is preposterous for numerous reasons, although most fundamentally because of the inconvenient fact that the Hollywood dog was already dead by the time Michaud's was conceived.

Regardless of his muddled parentage, the French Rin Tin Tin was talented enough to win a few starring roles. In the end, of course, he never ascended to the heights of his namesake. But if Michaud had hoped to create enough confusion to link the two, he succeeded beyond his wildest dreams, just not within his dog's lifetime. His Rin Tin Tin died in 1945. An article announcing the death appeared in the magazine *Ambiance* and included notice of his funeral at the Cimetière des Chiens, where he was buried under a modest grave marker.[18] The earliest accounts to mention a grave for Rin Tin Tin in Paris suddenly make sense. They date from only a few years later and display a curious lack of the enthusiasm one might expect for history's most famous dog.

Rin Tin Tin, seen on set in the 1920s, is still regarded
as history's most famous dog.

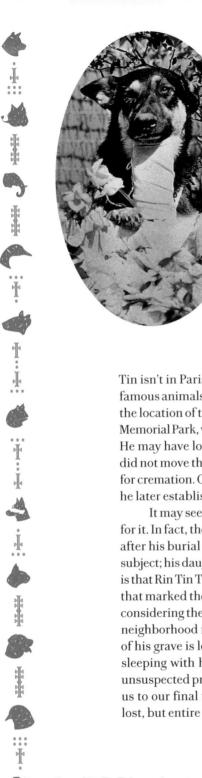

The first newspaper to make note of the grave, for example, does not do so until near the end of a story on the Cimetière des Chiens, and says nothing about the dog being a major Hollywood celebrity—since it was at that time understood that the dog buried there wasn't.[19] Over time, however, people forgot that a French Rin Tin Tin had existed, the cemetery changed ownership, and many of its documents were destroyed by a fire. Meanwhile, visitors to the cemetery reported on what they saw, unwitting journalists reported on what they heard, a considerably more substantial grave marker was installed courtesy of benefactors, and a dog who simply shared the name Rin Tin Tin morphed into the Rin Tin Tin.

All of this, of course, leads to an obvious question: if Rin Tin Tin isn't in Paris, where is he? Here we encounter an irony, because of all the famous animals whose graves we have located, in the end we are left to guess at the location of the most famous of all. One place he's not is the Los Angeles Pet Memorial Park, where a search of the records turns up nothing related to Duncan. He may have lost the Beverly Hills house soon after Rin Tin Tin died, but he did not move the casket to the pet cemetery, nor did he take the remains there for cremation. Could he have moved the grave elsewhere? Perhaps to the ranch he later established in Riverside, California, and spent the rest of his life at?

It may seem a tempting proposition, but there is absolutely no evidence for it. In fact, there is no evidence for anything involving Rin Tin Tin's remains after his burial in 1932. Duncan's surviving archives are entirely mum on the subject; his daughter likewise does not recall him mentioning it. The best guess is that Rin Tin Tin remained where he was originally interred. But with the cross that marked the spot now gone and the rosebush presumably withered—and considering the mercurial nature of Southern California real estate, the entire neighborhood may well have undergone radical change—the exact location of his grave is long forgotten. The world's most famous dog may very well be sleeping with his favorite toy exactly where he was laid to rest, an entirely unsuspected presence to those who walk above. Rin Tin Tin's lost grave brings us to our final topic, because it isn't just individual graves that can become lost, but entire pet cemeteries.

One of Rin Tin Tin's puppies rests chin and paws on the cross that marked his grave.

A Rin Tin Tin is interred in this grave in Paris—but not the one people think.

The End

The Death (and Rebirth)
of Pet Cemeteries

The pet cemetery at the Presidio in San Francisco is one of the rarest types of all: a survivor. Opened in 1952 on a picturesque plot surrounded by Scotch pines and overlooking the ocean, it was intended as a place for military families to bury their pets. It certainly looked military enough at first glance, with most of the graves marked by uniform wooden plaques with stenciled lettering. The spartan appearance was merely a veneer, however, as a unique brand of warmth showed through in the epitaphs. Puddin Dandridge, for instance, was a "Mean thing, rotten cat, but loved and missed by us all." Nearby was Snowflake, who "obeyed orders and answered to the CO's call," as well as Knucklehead, who was sent off as a "Parakeet to Paradise." Not everyone went in for jocular humor, however. The owners of Hula-Girl, for instance, broke ranks to offer a more simple and straightforward truth: "We know love, we had this little dog."

Confined to a small patch of land, the cemetery was nearly full within a decade. By the 1970s it had been closed to interments, and with the owners of the pets having moved on to other posts, it was also deteriorating. But as an adorable quirk in one of America's quirkiest cities, there were locals willing to help maintain it. A self-appointed caretaker tended the grounds, and a Boy Scout troop later took his place. But goodwill alone can only go so far. The Presidio had been decommissioned in 1994 and turned over to the National Parks Service. Almost no federal money went to the cemetery, but budget-conscious bureaucrats nevertheless took aim at it as an example of waste. "You have to ask yourself, 'Is a pet cemetery a historically significant structure?,'" a congressional aide complained. "I don't think the American people think their money should be spent on a pet cemetery."[1]

Of course, no one had actually bothered to ask the American people if that were indeed the case, and the grounds were instead classified as a "non-contributing feature" of the Presidio of San Francisco. In the lingo of the National Parks Service, this refers to a site that contributes no historical, cultural, or archeological value, and therefore lacks federal protection. Meanwhile, an adversary that had long loomed directly above the now vulnerable cemetery

finally prepared to strike. The little animal arcadia had been dwarfed from the start by the ominous presence of Doyle Drive, a section of roadway elevated on pillars that rose above the grounds to connect the city to the Golden Gate Bridge. Doyle Drive dated to 1938, and by the 1990s needed to be completely rebuilt. This was full demolition and reconstruction, right in the midst of the cemetery grounds.

In 2009, an orange safety fence was erected around the cemetery's perimeter. Work on the overpass began, with the grounds blocked off to the public and increasingly in tatters. The right words were said, the Presidio Trust having made an agreement with CalTrans that the pet cemetery should be preserved. But the right words had been said for many other pet cemeteries facing destruction, and had always proved hollow. Meanwhile, grave markers already fragile owing to the passage of time wound up overturned and broken, and entire rows of plots vanished under mudflow—a reminder of how history had shown time and again that love may be eternal, but pet cemeteries are not.

It is likely that as many pet cemeteries have failed as currently exist, and the list includes some historically significant names. Kanis Ruhe in New York was so well known that some people began using the term as a synonym for "pet cemetery," yet it fell into anonymity by the 1930s and then simply disappeared, its location marked on old maps but with not a trace of it surviving.[2] Even mighty Molesworth fell. Once the most prestigious animal burial ground in Britain, the last interment was in the 1950s, and the property was afterward left to the predations of scavengers, who carted off many of the stones to be

Extensive damage to the Presidio pet cemetery, 2014 photo. Small wonder many people feared for its future.

recycled as paving for patios. For years, no one was sure where the cemetery had even been, until the property was sold and the new owner discovered what was left, buried under thick overgrowth.

There are many similar stories of pet cemeteries reaching the end of their life spans and being reclaimed by nature. Their ruins then linger like skeletons in the weeds, waiting for urban explorers to rediscover the weathered remains. That pet cemeteries are so vulnerable is due to a combination of factors. Many are founded by people with big hearts but tiny wallets and no business plan. Their primary commodity is land, but if their lots are small, they have limited ability to generate income. Maintenance fees may not cover costs, making it impossible to keep up with deteriorating plots—many still-functioning facilities show signs of the strain, and it is not uncommon to find cracked and overturned gravestones, their promises that love once given will not be forgotten appearing as empty as a broken vase. Pet cemeteries are also highly susceptible to economic downturns. The Great Depression, for example, resulted in the first massive wave of pet cemetery closures, having cost them an estimated three-quarters of their business.[3]

Cemeteries for humans can effectively end up on life support. Even centuries beyond their last interments, they hang on thanks to regulations that protect their graves from being disturbed. Pet cemeteries, on the other hand, may be *terra sancta* to animal lovers, but not to bureaucracies. It is as if our legislative bodies have never gotten past the "only a dog" and "only a cat" days. In some cases, forward-thinking cemetery owners have taken precautions to protect their legacies. At Hartsdale, for instance, Dr. Johnson registered restrictions on his property's deed in 1914 to mandate that his successors maintain the site as an animal burial ground.[4] In the vast majority of cases, however, if a property is sold, the graves have virtually no protection against development. Local authorities may impose such steps as allowing a certain period of time during which plot holders have the option to move their pets' graves, but this will only forestall the bulldozers.

An example illustrating just how vulnerable pet cemeteries can be is found in Santa Cruz, California. Pine Knoll Pet Cemetery opened in 1937, but it was a mere two-acre property and eventually became filled. It then grew distressed as the pet owners themselves passed away and the surrounding forest proved an implacable adversary to the grounds. The land was valuable, however. Sold in 2002, an agreement was made that whatever graves were left unclaimed would be exhumed, with the remains interred in a mass pit. The property could then be developed for housing.[5]

Toppled headstone at a cemetery founded in 1910 alongside a Pittsburgh animal hospital.

THE END

Before the title had transferred, however, it was discovered that the land was home not only to deceased animals. The Mount Hermon June beetle, designated as endangered, also lived there. Facing a time-consuming bureaucratic process with no guarantee that they would be allowed to break ground, the buyers cancelled the sale. The pet cemetery was saved, but only continued to deteriorate. And its salvation came not thanks to the sixty-five years' worth of pets the ground had been entrusted with, but because someone found a three-quarter-inch insect there. This is not to mock the conservation efforts for the June beetle, its habitat should absolutely be respected. But it makes a definite point about the status of animal graves when several hundred of them were no deterrent to the property's development, yet a living beetle stopped the process dead in its tracks.

Certain pet cemeteries allow a person's cremation ashes to be placed in the same grave as a pet, however. Might statutes governing human burial sites act as a protective blanket if one of these pet cemeteries were to face the precipice? The answer is unknown and there are numerous mitigating regional factors, but the best evidence is not encouraging. The case likely to be tested first is in British Columbia, where at least two human burials are suspected at the Surrey Pet Cemetery, which was closed in the 1990s. Restrictions governing the land have lapsed, making it available to developers, and some have already begun drawing up plans. Before work could go forward the disposition of potential human graves would have to be settled, and according to local regulations a provincial director could be appointed to provide oversight, and would have the authority to add stipulations.[6] At the director's whim, it could be required that the graves of the pets be preserved. But once he or she is satisfied, construction could commence with the land legally no different than a vacant lot, and the current local opinion is that even human cremains wouldn't be a deterrent, only the discovery of human skeletal remains would.

The myriad vulnerabilities and long history of failure is why what happened under Doyle Drive at the Presidio is such a special case. When the big machines went to work and the little wooden markers fell into broken pieces, hopelessly cordoned off from loving hands that might

Distressed graves in New Orleans, Santa Cruz, Baltimore, and San Tan and Casa Grande, Arizona.

Nellie Blair, founder of defunct Surrey Pet Cemetery. Her cremains are believed to be interred there.

provide them with care, it is easy to see why many people felt this was the end. Consider that even Cherry's gravestone at Hyde Park has been destroyed. Those neighboring it still stand, but his grave is now marked only by a broken stone base. If the most historic marker of all had been allowed to decay beyond repair, what chance did those at the Presidio have? As a decade passed behind the orange fence, you couldn't blame the doubters who figured the graves would simply be ignored until they were forgotten.

But the doubters be damned. In 2019 the Presidio Trust, backed by private funds rather than public monies, went to work. As construction wound down, a secret weapon in the pet cemetery's fight for survival was brought forth. Measuring over four hundred pages, the *Preservation Maintenance Plan for the Pet Cemetery Presidio of San Francisco* was unlike any other document ever prepared.[7] Containing a wealth of photos, notes, and maps, it had been compiled before construction began, to provide extensive details of the 424 grave markers that had been present on the grounds. Using it as a guide, the Presidio staff now began reassembling the broken pieces like a giant jigsaw puzzle, returning them to where they had once stood.

Groundskeepers meanwhile began the task of replanting. And as a final and fitting touch, the public, who had for so long tended the cemetery to keep it

from falling into obscurity, was invited back to lend a hand. Volunteers descended on the property on a sunny autumn morning to repaint the white picket fence that, with the orange construction barricades removed, would again mark the cemetery's boundaries. And with that, and seemingly against all odds, the little pet cemetery was born anew.

Puddin Dandridge and Snowflake once more held court among the Scotch pines overlooking the Pacific Ocean. Knucklehead was back too, nestled in the long-dormant flowers now in bloom, as was Hula-Girl. And just inside the cemetery's gate was a sign, picked up from the ground and restored, proclaiming, "The love these animals gave will never be forgotten." The identity of who originally painted it and when have been lost to the passage of time, but the words have not. Now proudly set back in place, they are, at least in one case, a promise that has been kept.

The Presidio pet cemetery was reborn under the shadow of the overpass that threatened its destruction, and, with its grave markers reconstructed, it again pays tribute to the animals laid to rest there.

ENDNOTES

INTRODUCTION

1   On Cherry, see E. A. Brayley Hodgetts, "A Cemetery for Dogs," *Strand*, July 1893, 625–633.
2   The gravestone is in the collection of the Getty Villa, Los Angeles.
3   "Wo liegt der Hund begraben?," *Der Erzähler: Ein Unterhaltersblatt für Jedermann* 52, June 28, 1856, 207; George Frederick Pardon, *Dogs: Their Sagacity, Instincts, and Uses* (London: Blackwood, 1857), 246; "Winterstein (I)," http://www.suehnekreuz.de/thueringen/winterstein.htm.
4   On these two dogs, see "Wo liegt der Hund begraben?," 207; Pardon, *Dogs*, 246; "Winterstein (I)"; Ria Hörter, "Dog Statues: Pug Memorial in Winnenden, Germany," *The Canine Chronicle Annual*, 2017–2018, 228–229.
5   Walter L. Chaney, "The True Story of 'Old Drum,'" *Breeder's Gazette*, December 16, 1915, 1094, 1085, 1170, 1176. Chaney's is the fullest surviving account, based upon trial records that are now lost.
6   "Prefer Dogs to Babies," *Latter Day Saints' Millenial Star*, May 2, 1907, 297–298.

CHAPTER I

1   E. A. Brayley Hodgetts, "A Cemetery for Dogs," *Strand*, July 1893, 625.
2   "Our London Letter," *Birmingham and Aston Chronicle*, March 6, 1886, 3.
3   Statistics regarding cleanup fees are from Edouard Charles, "A Cemetery for Animals," *Strand*, July 1901, 715.
4   "A Cat's Funeral," *Edinburgh Evening News*, September 17, 1885, 3.
5   "A Dog Funeral," *Midland Daily Telegraph*, May 22, 1899, 3; "Dog Funeral," *Daily Mail*, May 22, 1899, 3.
6   "Cosy Corner Chat," *Gentlewoman*, April 22, 1899, 533.
7   William G. Fitzgerald, "Dandy Dogs," *Strand*, January 1896, 550.
8   Quoted in Augustus J. C. Hare, *The Story of My Life: Volume 4, 5, 6* (Frankfurt: Outlook Verlag, 2020), 241.
9   Quoted in "Of Dead Dogs," *Graphic: An Illustrated Weekly Newspaper*, March 31, 1883, 343.
10 "A Dog's Funeral," *Portsmouth Evening News*, August 17, 1880, 3.
11 Jan Bondeson, *Amazing Dogs: A Cabinet of Canine Curiosities* (Gloucestershire: Amberly, 2013), 257.
12 "A Dog's Cemetery," *Birmingham Gazette and Express*, August 20, 1906, 4.
13 *The Gentlewoman*, October 6, 1894, 422.
14 "The Dog's Acre in Hyde Park," *Sketch*, March 8, 1899, 300; Hodgetts, "A Cemetery for Dogs," 625, 633.
15 Moussoo's epitaph is adapted from a 19th-century poem by George Whyte-Melville, "The Place Where the Old Horse Died."
16 "The Grave of a Cat," *Washington Evening Times*, February 25, 1899, 3.
17 "Some Londoners' Little Worries," *Folkestone Express*, October 19, 1902, 5. Other accounts claim the curse was Coptic; see "London's Dog Cemetery," *Washington Post*, August 19, 1907, 6.
18 All surviving documentation relating to the pet cemetery at Molesworth, including copies of burial records and miscellaneous press clippings, is preserved at the Huntingdon Library and Archives.
19 "A Touching Ceremony," *Salisbury and Wilton Times*, August 17, 1900, 7.
20 Hodgetts, "A Cemetery for Dogs," 629.
21 *Ibid*.
22 *Ibid*. The photo of Topper appears on the same page.
23 George B. Taylor, *Man's Friend, the Dog* (New York: Stokes, 1891), 7.
24 "A Dog's Cemetery," 4. No proof exists that either Victoria or Alexandra had pets in Hyde Park, but it became a persistent part of the mythology. See, for instance, "The London Dog Cemetery," *Philadelphia Inquirer*, October 8, 1899, 4:3.

25 See "Dog Ground in Berlin," *Dover Western Times*, April 4, 1898, 4; "German's Fear for Kaiser's Safety" (German correspondence), *Brooklyn Daily Eagle*, August 26, 1900, 11; Bondeson, *Amazing Dogs*, 255.
26 "Queer Dog Cemetery," *New Britain Daily Herald*, December 26, 1925, 16. On the destruction of the cemetery, see "Berlin Dog Cemetery Goes," *New York Times*, November 26, 1927, 7.
27 The quote is a translation of an excerpt from *Das Schwarze Korps* (The Black Corps), a publication for SS members. The translation appeared in "Nazis and Dog Cemeteries," *Observer*, October 27, 1935, 16.
28 My translation, from a quote in Laurent Lasne, *L'île aux chiens* (Bois-Colombes: Val-Arno, 1988), 37–38, 53. Lasne's book is also the most comprehensive source for the early history of the cemetery.
29 "Dog Worship in Paris," *Chicago Tribune*, December 17, 1899, 41.
30 In *Amazing Dogs*, 191–192, Bondeson includes a section on Barry, and specifically mentions that he had been sent to Bern to live out the last two years of his life.
31 On the earliest burials, see Lasne, *L'île aux chiens*, 57, note 63.
32 The English translation of the card is taken from "Dog Worship in Paris." The incident with Bijou is mentioned in Lasne, *L'île aux chiens*, 66, and Anna Huntington Smith, *Cemeteries for Animals, Ancient and Modern, and the Life Beyond* (Boston: Animal Rescue League, 1913), 4.
33 "Imposing Cemetery for Dogs Marks Paris Tribute to Pets," *Washington Post*, September 26, 1920, 4:3.

CHAPTER II

1   "Dog Digs Own Grave, Then Dies," *New York Times*, June 9, 1926, 37.
2   That these are dumping grounds is made clear by the context in which the term was used. See, for example, "Council Proceedings," *Newton Daily Kansan*, June 8, 1893, 4, which mentions establishing a "dog cemetery and garbage dumping ground."
3   "Twenty Five Years Ago, How the Big Moose Lake Copper Mine was Discovered, Digging a Dog's Grave," *Anaconda Standard*, January 1, 1899, 12.
4   "A Dog's Obsequies," *Rome Daily Sentinel*, August 31, 1883, 1.
5   "Burial of a Cat," *Brooklyn Daily Eagle*, February 9, 1899, 7.
6   See "Burial of Pet Dog Causes Uproar in Pana," *Chicago Tribune*, May 23, 1938, 1; "Interment of Fritzi," *St. Louis Post-Dispatch*, March 28, 1909, 55; "Clash Over a Dog's Grave," *Kansas City Star* (Evening Edition), March 3, 1909, 1; "Will Trial Putting on the Dog," *Los Angeles Times*, October 20, 1927, 2.
7   "Dogolatry," *Catholic Union and Times*, July 23, 1888, 6. For more on Cosey Bell, see "Cosey Bell's Coffin," *Boston Globe*, August 15, 1888, 5; "Cosey Bell's Funeral," *Chicago Tribune*, August 15, 1888, 5; "Poor Cosey Bell's Bones," *New York Evening World*, September 6, 1888, 4; "A Bad Dog Turned Out," *Buffalo Lightning Express*, September 7, 1888, 10; "1888: Cosey Bell, the Skye Terrier Almost Buried at Woodlawn Cemetery, Bronx," https://hatchingcatnyc.com/2019/09/11/cozey-bell-woodlawn-cemetery/, posted September 11, 2019.
8   "Dogolatry," 6.
9   The article was syndicated around the country, usually titled "Cemetery for Dogs," although sometimes it ran untitled. See, for example, *Cherryvale Daily News*, March 19, 1896, 2.
10 This is how the story is told in the cemetery's own book, for example. See Edward C. Martin, Jr., *Dr. Johnson's Apple Orchard: The Story of America's First Pet Cemetery* (Hartsdale Canine Cemetery, 1997), 12. There is nothing insidious in the book neglecting to mention Emily Berthet; at the time of publication, her role in the founding had been forgotten.
11 Thanks to Mary Thurston, Hartsdale's historian, for her generosity in offering me the information on the Emily Berthet saga from her archival research.

12 "A Dog and Cat Cemetery: New York Now Has a Place to Bury Its Dead Pets," *New York Sun*, October 16, 1898, 3:7. Another article appeared on October 30 in the *New York World*. Not much more is known of Emily Berthet. Additional information can be found in a flier for Hartsdale Heritage Fund, written by Mary Thurston for their 2021 annual drive, "Hartsdale Pet Cemetery: A Look Back."

13 "Costly Burial of a Dog," *Buffalo Evening News*, July 20, 1900, 6. This article identified the dog as a collie, but other early histories claim him as a spaniel; see Sarah Knowles Bolton, *Our Devoted Friend the Dog* (Boston: LC Page, 1902), 360–362.

14 "Where New York's 'Smart Dogs' Find Final Last Place," *New York Times*, September 3, 1905, 3:3.

15 "A Dog Heaven Where There Are Over 3000 Friends of Man Buried," *Central New Jersey Home News*, July 11, 1920, 9.

16 "Where New York's 'Smart Dogs' Find Final Last Place," 3:3.

17 "Cemetery for Dogs and Cats," *Pittsburgh Daily Post*, May 20, 1906, 4:2.

18 "Dog Cemetery," *Mt. Vernon Daily Argus*, April 22, 1905, 4.

19 As vernacular for a common mutt, "jes' dog" had been in use since at least the turn of the century. On Grumpy, see also Doug Keister, *Stories in Stone New York: A Field Guide to New York City Area Cemeteries & Their Residents* (Layton, UT: Gibbs Smith, 2011), 192; "1926: Grumpy, 'Jes' an Ordinary, Plain, Everyday Dog' of a New York Banker," https://hatching-catnyc.com/2016/06/30/grumpy-ordinary-everyday-dog/, posted June 30, 2016.

20 On Rex Moore, see "A Monument to Her Adored Poodle—Nothing for Her Mother," *Philadelphia Inquirer Magazine*, April 20, 1930, 8; "Devotion Honored at Pet Cemetery," *Mt. Vernon Argus*, August 5, 1952, 7; "1919: Rex Moore, the St. Bernard Who Still Stands Post in the West Bronx," https://hatchingcatnyc.com/2014/12/14/rex-moore-st-bernard-bronx/, posted December 14, 2014.

21 "Hartsdale Canine Cemetery Most Imposing of Its Kind in America," *New York Herald*, June 29, 1919, 70. See also "13,000 to Bury a Dog," *New York Daily News*, June 25, 1912, 17.

22 "A New Yorker at Large," *Spokane Spokesman-Review*, April 23, 1929, 4; "Ashes of 3 Scions of '400' to Rest in Dog Cemetery," *Camden Morning Post*, March 24, 1928, 2.

23 "A Monument to Her Adored Poodle," 8.

24 Bolton, 362; "A Dog Cemetery and Horse Haven," *Standard Union*, September 1, 1900, 9.

25 The quote is from a classified ad placed by Miller in the *New York Sun*, April 19, 1908, 10. For contemporary accounts of Kanis Ruhe, see Anna Huntingdon Smith, *Cemeteries for Animals, Ancient and Modern, and the Life Beyond* (Boston: Aniam Rescue League, 1913), 12; "Maxine Elliott and her Dog Sport," *Buffalo Courier*, April 10, 1910, 16; "New York Has Cemetery for Dogs and Cats Where Each Has Tombstone with an Original Epitaph," *New York Press*, January 4, 1914, 9; "How Brindle Broke into Society," *St. Louis Star and Times All American Magazine*, April 18, 1914, 2.

26 "New York Has Cemetery for Dogs and Cats," 9.

27 *Ibid.*

28 *Ibid.*

29 "Buried Like a Dog," *Rochester Democrat and Chronicle*, January 10, 1901, 3.

30 The cemetery was called Dell Wood or Dellwood. See "Buried Like a Dog," 3.

31 For reports on Nightlife's funeral, see "2000 at Rites for 'Nightlife,' Killed by Car," *Central New Jersey Home News*, November 28, 1952, 1; "Nightlife, Mongrel Dog, Goes to Rest as Thousands Mourn," *Chicago Tribune*, November 29, 1952, 9; "Rich Funeral Given Nightlife," *Norfolk Virginian-Pilot*, November 30, 1952, 5:15; "400 Attend Funeral of Resort Mongrel," *Paterson News*, December 1, 1952, 16.

32 The quote has frequently been attributed to Harry Truman but has in fact been around since at least 1911. Ralph Keyes, *The Quote Verifier: Who Said What, Where, When* (New York: St. Martin's, 2006), 47.

33 "Unique Cemetery for Capitol Pets," *Los Angeles Times*, June 22, 1902, 10. See also "Abode of Dead Pets," *Washington Post*, August 2, 1914, 28.

34 On the history of Aspin Hill, see especially Julianne Mangin, "Aspin Hill Pet Cemetery: 100 Years of Pets, People, and the Stories Behind the Stones," *Montgomery County Story* 63:2, 2020, 6.

35 The last sentence of the epitaph is taken from "My Dog," a canine eulogy by St. John Lucas, *New Poems* (Constable: London, 1908), 85–86.

36 The 1924 founding of Brown Pet Cemetery, which still exists, is noted in "A Cemetery for Pets," *Indianapolis Star*, October 1, 1939, 78. On other animal cemeteries in the Midwest, see "Curious Cemeteries for Animal Pets," *Park and Cemetery and Landscape Gardening* 22:1, March 1912, 50; "Dog Cemetery for Chicago," *Coffeyville Daily Journal*, December 18, 1915, 7; "Dog Graveyard Stands in Memory of Those That Saved Human Lives," *Chicago Suburbanite Economist*, August 16, 1931, 2; "Fond Owners Place Pets to Rest in Cemetery in Clarendon Hills," *Chicago Tribune*, January 25, 1953, 3:1.

37 "Great Hearted Bobbie Dead," *Oregon Daily Journal*, April 4, 1927, 1. See also "Bobbie, Wonder Dog Dies in Hospital of Ptomaine Poisoning," *Salem Capital Journal*, April 4, 1927, 1; "Child's Casket Is Provided for Wonder Canine," *Salem Capital Journal*, April 6, 1927, 2; "Famous Silverton Dog's Exploit Is Recalled for State Fair Guests," *Salem Capital Journal*, August 31, 1933, 6; the "Bobbie the Wonder Dog Scrapbooks" in the Oregon Historical Society Research Library.

CHAPTER III

1 The original version is attributed to Linda Barnes and was written specifically to commemorate a cat, with versions then being adapted for dogs and pets in general.

2 The origin of the poem has been debated, but it seems clear that the original author is Clare Horner. The poem appears under her name in the *Kansas City Times*, February 8, 1935, 18, which reprinted it from the poetry journal *The Gypsy*. Its title at that time was "Immortality."

3 Edna Clyne is now Edna Clyne-Rekhy. On the history of "Rainbow Bridge," see Paul Koudounaris, "The Rainbow Bridge: The True Story Behind History's Most Influential Piece of Animal Mourning Literature," https://www.orderofthegooddeath.com/article/the-rainbow-bridge-the-true-story-behind-historys-most-influential-piece-of-animal-mourning-literature/, posted February 9, 2023.

4 Anna Huntington Smith, *Cemeteries for Animals, Ancient and Modern, and the Life Beyond* (Boston: Animal Rescue League, 1913), 5.

5 "Iconic Photos of Animals Throughout History," https://cheezburger.com/15117061/iconic-photos-of-animals-throughout-history-viral-tweets, posted July 1, 2021.

6 "New England's Only Cemetery for Pets," *Boston Globe*, December 26, 1920, 52.

7 "Honor Memory of Cat and Dog Pets in Dedham," *Boston Post*, January 11, 1921, 9.

8 Eva J. DeMarsh, "Only a Cat," *Our Dumb Animals* 51:7, December, 1918, 110.

9 *First Series of Butler's Poetical Sketches* (New York: self-published, 1870), 27.

10 *Ibid.*, 55.

11 *Ibid.*, 47. The poem was titled "Epitaph on a King Charles Spaniel. Property of Doctor Elliot. Cujas Conis est!"

12 W. B. L, "Only a Dog," *Vermont Journal*, August 26, 1876, 3.

13 It seems that the poem was first published in the *St. Louis Daily Globe-Democrat* on Sunday, February 4, 1900, 3:12.

14 It appeared on page 2 of the February 15, 1881, edition under the title "Flight," and was listed as an obituary dated January 1, 1881.

15 That "S.M.A.C." is Collins is thanks to *Publisher's Weekly*, April 22, 1882, 433, which confirmed that those initials were used by her—she was at the time a known, published author.

16 *Fanciers Journal* 5:2, July 12, 1890, 23.

17 "A Headstone for a Dog," *Brooklyn Daily Eagle*, February 10, 1889, 1. For background on the incident with Fannie, see "1881: An Ode to Fannie Howe, Only a Dog Who Lies in Green-Wood Cemetery," https://hatchingcatnyc.com/2015/04/19/fannie-howe-only-a-dog-green-wood-cemetery/, posted April 19, 2015.

18 See "Honors to a Dead Dog," *Washington D.C. Evening Star*, November 29, 1879, 6. The claim that the dog was twenty-three is found in "Buried in the Family Plot," *New York Herald*, November 25, 1879, 5.

19 A long-time resident of the area reports that the cemetery was abandoned in the 1990s, and that the cat's epitaph was originally inscribed on a wooden plaque, which was later replaced with one in stone. The inscription remained the same.

20 Mrs. H. B. B. Paull, *Only A Cat; or, The Autobiography of Tom Blackman, A favourite Cat which lived seventeen years with the same family, dying at last of old age* (London: Elliot Stock, 1876), 1.

21 The poem began to appear in the Midwest in July 1890; see, for example, *Davenport Daily Times*, July 10, 4. It continued to be reprinted for over a decade.

22 The poem appeared in *Our Dumb Animals* 32:4, September 1899, 51. During the next decade it would be widely syndicated around the United States.

23 Paull, *Only A Cat*, 7.

24 The poem first appeared in the *Delphos Daily Herald*, February 16, 1896, 6, and began circulating the following week, often alongside an illustration of a mother cat looking on as a girl holds a bag filled with kittens.

25 The poem was originally published in *Our Dumb Animals* 36:2, July, 1903, 25.

26 That Mrs. Jones was Lillian M. Dowse can be confirmed through many sources. See, for example, her husband's obituary in the *Greenfield Recorder*, August 12, 1908, 2. Mrs. Jones served as both a secretary and a director of the Animal Rescue League. See "Animal Rescue League," *Boston Globe*, February 7, 1900, 5, and "Cared for 5131 Animals," *Boston Globe*, February 6, 1901, 7.

27 "To Dumb Heroes and Friends," *Boston Globe*, September 5, 1915, 50.

28 "Second Try at Death," *Boston Globe*, May 6, 1903, 4.

29 "Poisoned Man Rang the Bell," *Boston Post*, May 1, 1903, 10.

30 The document is filed as Return of Death permit number 4800. It bears a stamp with the date May 20, and a second stamp registering it on May 21.

31 For the record of donations, see the *Annual Report of the Animal Rescue League of Boston* for 1910-1912 in the Collection of Circulars and Pamphlets in the New York Public Library.

32 "To Dumb Heroes and Friends," 50.

CHAPTER IV

1 "Soldier Got a Lift but Left Suitcase—Because of a Lion," *Los Angeles Times*, April 8, 1942, 2:1. Similar notices appeared on the same day in the *Pasadena Star-News, Pomona Progress-Bulletin*, and the *Hollywood Citizen News*.

2 Press notices on the story of Mary and her lion include "Court Debates Legal Status of Jungle Pets," *Hollywood Citizen-News*, November 19, 1937, 3; Leo Baron, "Troubles of Lion Owner Presented in City Court," *San Bernardino County Sun*, November 21, 1937, 4; "Neighbors Protest Full Grown Lions Cavorting in Owner's Backyard," *Van Nuys News*, November 22,

1937; Alma Whitaker, "Sugar and Spice," *Los Angeles Times*, April 30, 1937, 30; "Pet Lion Dies of Old Age; Given Honor Burial," *Evening Vanguard*, February 9, 1940, 6; "Woman's Pet Lion Succumbs to Old Age," *Los Angeles Times*, February 9, 1940, 21. Confirmation that Tawny had been used by MGM comes from Mary's court hearing on the noise complaint—there was an official studio list of Leo the Lions, and his name is not on it, but in explaining her sources of income, the rental of the lion to MGM was noted.

3 The dog is still commonly reported online as Petey. See Julianne Mangin, "Aspin Hill Pet Cemetery: 100 Years of Pets, People, and the Stories Behind the Stones," *Montgomery County Story* 63:2, 2020, 10.

4 Obera H. Rawles, "Hollywood's Amazing Cemetery for Pets of the Stars," *Salt Lake City Tribune Sunday Magazine*, January 24, 1937, 7.

5 On the ban, see "Pet Cemeteries Now Prohibited," *Van Nuys News*, July 20, 1928, 2. For a galling case of prosecution, see "Story of a Dog," *Los Angeles Record*, September 15, 1897, 3; "Moving Tale of a Dog," *Los Angeles Times*, September 16, 1896, 8; "Local News Briefed," *Los Angeles Record*, September 17, 1897, 4.

6 Mutt's name is also sometimes spelled Mut. He is also referred to by his film name, Scraps.

7 That the grave marker was a shoe is mentioned in "Chaplin's Famous Little Dog Is Dead," *Motography*, May 25, 1918, 1,000.

8 On the burial of the horse, see *Huell Howser's California Gold: Pet Cemetery* (documentary), KCET Los Angeles, broadcast September 3, 2007. The property was later developed as a Whole Foods 365.

9 For general background information on the Los Angeles Pet Memorial Park, see *Huell Howser's California Gold*, plus various articles spanning several decades: Nora Laing, "Where Sleeping Dogs Lie," *Los Angeles Times*, October 16, 1932, 11; Jean Jacques, "Pets of Famous Folks Are Buried in Unique Southern California Cemetery," *Santa Maria Times*, April 11, 1936, 6; Philip K. Scheuer, "Film Stars' Pets Interred in Fully-Equipped Cemetery," *Los Angeles Times*, April 19, 1936, 2:1; Rawles, "Hollywood's Amazing Cemetery for Pets of the Stars," 7; Aline Mosby, "Stars Bury Their Pets in Style," *Detroit Free Press*, December 5, 1948, 4:24; Steve Harvey, "Pets Get Devotion, Too," *Los Angeles Times*, April 28, 1976, 4:1; Cecilia Rasmussen, "Veterinarian to the Stars Brought Pet Cemetery to Life," *Los Angeles Times*, April 20, 2003, 2:1.

10 "Veteran Shoots Stepson and Another, Then Turns Gun on Himself When Facing Arrest," *Los Angeles Times*, October 21, 1929, 2:2. Hornsby is mentioned as the president of the cemetery in "Chief's Dog Buried," *Los Angeles Evening Citizen News*, February 9, 1929, 2.

11 See "Beesemyer Cemetery Sued," *Los Angeles Evening Express*, April 18, 1931, 2:1; "Trouble Invades Pets' Happy Hunting Grounds," *Los Angeles Times*, April 18, 1931, 2:3; "Park to Continue as Animal Cemetery," *Los Angeles Times*, December 9, 1931, 2:5. On Nicola de Pento, see "Pet Funerals Depress Man and Property," *Los Angeles Evening Express*, September 6, 1929, 9; his rocking horse patent was filed in 1928, number 1,718,637.

12 That Mae West did not attend the funeral because she did not want to face cameras was reported in "Behind the Scenes in Hollywood," *Pittsburgh Sun-Telegraph*, October 5, 1933, 28.

13 "Chimpanzee Actor Dies; Funeral Planned for Today," *Los Angeles Times*, March 2, 1938, 2:3.

14 The bird was also known as Yves. Word of the funeral was carried by Associated Press. See, for example, "'Yes-Man' Parrot of De Mille Dies," *Salem Statesman-Journal*, September 17, 1937, 1.

15 For the funeral notice mentioning the tooth infection, see "Puzzums Rites Set for Today," *Los Angeles Times*, August 19, 1934, 5. The publicists were too late to get the spider story into his obituaries, but it did find its way into later accounts;

see Rawles. The story was also told as far away as Australia; see Julia MacDonald, "They Bury the Pets of the Film Stars in State," *Adelaide Advertiser*, July 4, 1936, 12.

16 Photos of Dumpsie going over the hurdles were sent out along the press wires; see "Camera Record of the Day News," *Wilmington Morning News*, April 13, 1932, 16. For the reference to Dumpsie being able to do "anything but card tricks," see Eileen Percy, "Carillo Plays New Gangster Role; Boles Still in Cast of Opera Singer," *Los Angeles Evening Express*, June 8, 1931, 15.

17 "Poisoner Kills Dumpsie, Toy Dog of the Screen," *Los Angeles Times*, November 15, 1934, 2:2.

18 "Lower Than the Beasts," *Los Angeles Times*, November 19, 1934, 2:4.

19 Many articles on the cemetery are heavily invested in the story of Kabar; see, for instance, Laing, "Where Sleeping Dogs Lie," and Scheuer, "Film Stars' Pets Interred in Fully-Equipped Cemetery." The story of Kabar's ghost eventually made the newspapers; see Susan King, "Restless Spirits," *Los Angeles Times*, October 31, 2011, 4:3. Mostly, however, it is found in books on hauntings, such as Janice Oberding, *The Big Book of California Ghost Stories* (London: Globe Pequot, 2021), 125, and on the Internet.

20 The phantom Kabar jumping through a window was claimed to have been seen at a séance celebrating Valentino's birthday. See Paul Lieberman, "Seeking the Soul of the Billion Dollar Butler," *Los Angeles Times Magazine* (newspaper supplement), May 18, 1997, 8.

21 Photos of Lassie Junior laying his paw on the grave were published in both "Dog Hero Gets 'Lassie' Award," *Gardena Valley News*, November 7, 1957, 34, and "Skippy, Dog Who Was War Hero, Gets Posthumous Lassie Award," *Torrance Herald*, November 3, 1957, 2. For Skippy receiving honors at City Hall, see "K-9 Corps Vets Honored by City," *Southwest Wave*, September 20, 1945, 1. For notice of his funeral, see "Canine Hero Given Final Rites," *Southwest Wave*, March 6, 1949, 1.

22 The murder the dog witnessed was of Jack Whalen, and Cohen's attorney was allowed to take him home from the station; see "Police Jail Cohen in Café Slaying," *Los Angeles Times*, December 5, 1959, 1. On the dognapping, see "Mickey Cohen's Dog Dognapped!," *Hollywood Citizen-News*, March 26, 1960, 1; for his return, see "All's Well Now—Cohen Has Mickey Jr. Back," *Los Angeles Times*, March 27, 1960, 4. The actor was Max Baer, Jr. The dog was killed by a driver who apparently pulled up onto the sidewalk to hit him, although accounts vary and were kept deliberately opaque. News of the death appeared on June 24, 1960; for example, "Mickey Cohen's Dog Killed," *Los Angeles Times*, 1.

23 Jeffrey Vallance issued a book, *Blinky: The Friendly Hen* (Los Angeles: Smart Art Press, 1979), which has seen updated editions, the last in 2019. There has been extensive commentary on Blinky, with Vallance discussing the episode on radio, on television, and in California periodicals. See in particular Bob Greene, "Saga of Blinky: A Man's Best Hen," *Sacramento Bee*, October 24, 1983, 17; Kevin Allman, "The Years of Blinky," *Los Angeles Times* (Calendar), June 18, 1989, 92; Patricia Ward Biederman, "The Valley Is His First Louvre," *Los Angeles Times* (Valley Edition), November 20, 1995, 6:1; Hunter Drohojoska-Philip, "60 Seconds With Jeffrey Vallance," *Los Angeles Times* (Calendar), March 6, 2008, 11.

CHAPTER V

1 Gonzalo Fernández de Oviedo y Valdés, *The Conquest and Settlement of the Island of Boriquen or Puerto Rico*, trans. and ed. Daymond Turner (Avon, CT: Limited Editions Club, 1975), 44–45. Becerrillo is mentioned in numerous books on war dogs, including Mary Elizabeth Thurston, *Lost History of the Canine Race: Our 15,000-Year Love Affair with Dogs* (Kansas

City, MO: Andrews McMeel, 1996), 85–86.

2 There are many accounts of Moustache's career, mostly compiled from early 19th-century sources, in particular, "Moustache: A Military Sketch," *Tales of the Wars; or, Naval and Military Chronicle*, April 1, 1837, 102–110.

3 There is no single primary source for Bob's career, but he is mentioned in many books on war dogs and discussed in Jan Toms, *Animal Graves and Memorials* (Buckinghamshire, UK: Shire, 2006), 76–77.

4 There is no shortage of published references to Bobbie's life and career. See, in particular, Nigel Cawthorne, *Canine Commandos: The Heroism, Devotion, and Sacrifice of Dogs in War* (Berkeley, CA: Ulysses Press, 2012), 26–32, and Jilly Cooper, *Animals in War* (London: Heinemann, 1983), 191.

5 The film, *Sgt. Stubby: An American Hero*, was released in April 2018 by Fun Academy Motion Pictures.

6 "War Dog Memorial," *New York Times*, November 23, 1919, 10:3. The eventual sculpture was based on a design submitted through a public competition by Walter Buttendorf and cast by Robert Caterson.

7 There are two published biographies of Rags. The one released during his lifetime is Jack Rohan, *Rags: The Story of a Dog Who Went to War* (New York: Grosset & Dunlap, 1930). There is also Grant Hayter-Menzies, *From Stray Dog to World War I Hero: The Paris Terrier Who Joined the First Division* (Lincoln, NB: Potomac Books, 2015). Rags's press clippings during his lifetime were voluminous.

8 "Pedigree," *York Daily Record*, October 13, 1925, 4.

9 Bill Wynne wrote a biography of Smoky, *Yorkie Doodle Dandy: A Memoir* (Mansfield, OH: Wynnesome Press, 1996). Another biography of Smoky is Nigel Allsop, *Smoky the War Dog: How a Tiny Yorkshire Terrier Became a Hero on the Front Line* (Wahroonga, NSW: New Holland Publishers, 2014). After Smoky died, Wynne was contacted by a woman who told him she had lost a Yorkshire terrier in New Guinea. If the story is true, it is the most likely explanation for Smoky's presence on the island.

10 There is no published biography of Sarge, but there are several press clippings covering the end of his life and his funeral. See the following articles from the *Los Angeles Mirror*: Frank Holdenried, "War Hero Dog Gets His Day," April 15, 1961, 10, and "Sarge,' War Dog Hero, Dies at 20," May 18, 1961, 1. The most important piece of reference material, however, is an unpublished account of his life by Jeanne Platt.

11 For background on Maria Dickin and the PDSA, see "Our History," https://secure.pdsa.org.uk/stories/our-history/.

12 The cat was technically Peter III. For background on Peter and the office of Chief Mouser, see "The Bureaucats at the Heart of Government," https://blog.nationalarchives.gov.uk/bureau-cats-heart-government/, posted June 7, 2016; and "Bureau-cats: A Short History of Whitehall's Official Felines," https://media.nationalarchives.gov.uk/index.php/bureau-cats/, posted March 29, 2017.

13 There is confusion over the number of Dickin recipients due to medals being issued to groups of animals involved in a single operation, and another medal awarded by the PDSA, the Gold Medal, which is the equivalent of the Dickin Medal for civilian animals. The PDSA considers the tally to be seventy-five. For the same reasons, there is confusion over the total number of Dickin Medal winners buried at Ilford, and once again I am using the PDSA's tally. The most comprehensive source on Dickin Medal winners is Peter Hawthorne, *The Animal Victoria Cross: The Dickin Medal* (Barnsley, UK: Pen & Sword, 2012).

14 Antis's owner is often listed as Václav Robert Bozdech, or sometimes just Robert. Bozdech himself used the first name Jan, however, including in a series of newspaper articles in which he recounted his life with Antis. I have followed

his example. His newspaper accounts ran over a series of Sundays in *The People*, on May 15, 22, and 29, and June 5, 12, and 19, 1960. There is also a biography of Antis: Damien Lewis, *War Dog: The No-Man's-Land Puppy Who Took to the Skies* (London: Sphere, 2013).

15   The quote on Antis's grave is taken from a verse by the 19th-century Scottish poet John Gibson Lockhart.

16   Simon's biography appeared in a restrained account soon after his death: Vera Cooper, *Simon the Cat (H.M.S. Amethyst)* (London: Hutchinson, 1950). Other volumes to appear include Lynne Barrett-Lee, *Able Seacat Simon: The True Story of a Very Special Cat* (London: Simon & Schuster, 2016); Jacky Donovan, *Seacat Simon: The Little Cat Who Became a Big Hero* (KIM Publishing, 2016); and Marcus Sterne, *Simon the Sea Cat* (Bowker, 2018). These tend to mythologize Simon and are intended for children. I also wrote about Simon in *A Cat's Tale: A Journey Through Feline History* (New York: Holt, 2020), but the book was narrated by the character of a cat and is more editorialized than objective.

17   The Earl of Mount Edgcombe, president of the Plymouth PDSA, expressed this sentiment at a memorial on Simon's behalf, stating that "the poor cat, having lost his ship, friends, and liberty, felt that there was not much worth living for, and died of a broken heart." See "Amethyst Cat Set an Example to Humans," *Western Morning News*, April 14, 1950, 7, which also mentions Weston accepting the medal.

18   The information on the funeral and attendees comes from "Simon of the Amethyst is Buried," *Herald Express* (Town Edition), December 1, 1949, 1.

CHAPTER VI

1   "Toad Glowers at Coolidge!," *Muncie Evening Press*, May 4, 1928, 2.

2   "'Old Rip' Back Home," *Abilene Reporter News*, September 29, 1961, 1.

3   James Dabney, "Letter Reawakens 'Rip' Toad Legend," *Fort Worth Star-Telegram*, September 10, 1976, 4. The two 1970s photos are printed side by side.

4   "'Old Rip' Kidnapped," *Abilene Reporter News* (Evening Edition), September 27, 1961, 1.

5   Despite being extensively covered in his day, Shep's biography will always be fragmentary since nothing is known before he appeared at the station. Railroad staff sold a small booklet that was popular with tourists and has formed the basis for his story. The River and Plains Society of Fort Benton published an account of him in 1995: *Forever Faithful: The Story of Shep*, eds. John G. and Sue Lepley.

6   George R. Jesse, *Researches into the History of the British Dog*, vol. 2 (London: Hardwicke, 1866). The plate, from an original drawing by Jesse, is found after page 278.

7   Alexander "Sandy" Gillam, "Laying the University's Dogs to Rest," *UVA Magazine*, Fall 2013, archived at https://uvamagazine.org/articles/laying_the_universitys_dogs_to_rest.

8   For background on Mary of Exeter and the other Dickin Medal–winning pigeons, see Peter Hawthorne, *The Animal Victoria Cross: The Dickin Medal* (Barnsley, UK: Pen & Sword, 2012), part 7. The PDSA also has a pamphlet on Mary: "Mary of Exeter, DM 32."

9   Cher Ami, "Dear Friend" in French, is grammatically a masculine construction, but the bird was female.

10   For the most in-depth account of Stoney, see M. Jaynes, *Elephants Among Us: Two Performing Elephants in Twentieth Century America*, 2nd edn., ebook (Earth Books, 2017).

11   See the following, from the *Arizona Republic*: "Workers in Grove Discover 56 Greyhound Carcasses," January 5, 1992, 2:1; Joyce Valdez, "Carcasses of 7 More Dogs Found," January 6, 1992, 2:1; Joyce Valdez, "More Dog Carcasses Found in Grove,

Probe Underway," January 8, 1992, 2:1; Paul Davenport, "Probe in Slaughter of Dogs Intensifies—124 Buried," January 10, 1992, 2:4; Brett Whiting and Art Thomason, "Breeder Admits Dumping Race Dogs," February 28, 1992, 1.

12   Andy's tragedy was widely reported, especially in Nebraska. See the following from the *Lincoln Journal Star*: "Senseless Destructions: No Suspects in Slaying of Famous Footless Goose," October 22, 1991, 11; "Headstone Memorializes Andy, the Footless Goose," January 18, 1992, 18.

13   The Boulder City cemetery is the only one for which any appreciable history is preserved. See Mike Zapler, "Makeshift pet cemetery serves as final home for many Nevada family pets," *Reno Gazette Journal*, May 25, 2000, 3:5; Amy Alonso and Ed Komenda, "Here Lies Beast," *Reno Gazette Journal*, December 14, 2020, 1.

14   Susan Orlean, *Rin Tin Tin: The Life and the Legend* (New York: Simon & Schuster, 2011), 81.

15   See, for example, an unpublished document by Everett George Opie, a radio personality and producer who visited Duncan's home after the dog's death: "Rin Tin Tin Junior 'Carries On,'" Lee Duncan archives, Riverside Museum, California, box 4, folder 2.

16   Mimi Pinson, "Touissant: Le Cimetière des Chiens," *Parallèle* 50, November 5, 1948, 10.

17   Personal conversations with the author.

18   "Vedette à quatre pattes Rin-Tin-Tin est mort de chagrin," *Ambiance*, December 19, 1945, 6–7.

19   Pinson, "Le Cimetière des Chiens," 10.

THE END

1   Kim Boatman, "Military Pets of Past Spend Eternity in Presidio Cemetery," *Sacramento Bee*, August 25, 1993, 2:4.

2   "A 'Kanis Ruhe' is among us" was how a pet cemetery near Chicago was announced in "Pets to Have Nice Green Cemetery," *Des Moines Register and Leader* (cartoon section), December 26, 1915, 2. Kanis Ruhe is labeled on maps held at the Yorktown Museum, dated 1911 and 1930.

3   "The Depression Hits the Dog Cemeteries," *American Weekly*, March 26, 1933, 6.

4   Deed restrictions were registered in both 1914 and 1916. The question may arise about whether a deed restricting a plot as a pet cemetery can be circumvented. There is no simple answer. Such a deed restriction is enforceable and not necessarily easy to remove, but it can be challenged, and there are some circumstances, such as if the property were declared eminent domain, in which it would be extinguished.

5   On the sale, closure, and cancellation of the sale of Pine Knoll, see the following in the *Santa Cruz Sentinel*: public notice on June 29, 2002, 2:4; Dan White, "Pet Cemetery, R.I.P.," July 2, 2002, 1; Jeanene Harlick, "Beetle, Flower, Halt Pet Cemetery Move," August 1, 2002, 1.

6   The relevant regulations are Part 10 of the British Columbia Cremation, Interment, and Funeral Services Act, and Section 26 of the Regulation Regarding Conversion and Closure of a Place of Interment. Thanks to Heather Kamitakahara at the City of Surrey for the most up-to-date information as this book was going to press.

7   *Preservation Maintenance Plan for the Pet Cemetery Presidio of San Francisco* (Presidio Trust, 2007). A copy is available online at https://p.widencdn.net/9tljrt.

SOURCES OF ILLUSTRATIONS

All photographs by the author and all archive images from the author's personal collection unless otherwise stated below.

Every effort has been made to locate and credit copyright holders of the material reproduced in this book. The author and publisher apologize for any omissions or errors, which can be corrected in future editions.

a=above, **b**=below, **c**=center, **l**=left, **r**=right

12. Missouri State Archives;
13. Archive PL/Alamy Stock Photo;
14. Topfoto;
18. Donald Macleish, Hyde Park Cemetery, *Wonderful London*, St John Adcock (Ed.), 1927;
21. Courtesy of Paul Frecker;
22. Fitz W. Guerin/Library of Congress Prints and Photographs Division;
31. Edmund F. Arras Collection/Columbus Metropolitan Library;
38. **t.** Huntingdon Library and Archives;
38. **b.** Huntingdon Library and Archives;
39. Huntingdon Library and Archives;
42. akg-images/TT News Agency/SVT Keystone View Company/SVT;
51. akg-images/ullstein bild;
54. **t.** The U.S. National Archives and Records Administration(306-NT-365F-1);
54. **b.** The U.S. National Archives and Records Administration (306-NT-365F-2);
55. George Grantham Bain Collection/Library of Congress Prints and Photographs Division;
58. **tl.** George Grantham Bain Collection/Library of Congress Prints and Photographs Division;
58. **tr.** George Grantham Bain Collection/Library of Congress Prints and Photographs Division;
58. **b.** George Grantham Bain Collection/Library of Congress Prints and Photographs Division;
59. Daniel Frasnay/akg-images;
63. National Photo Company Collection/Library of Congress Prints and Photographs Division;
66. **t.** Wyoming State Archives Photo Collection;
68. Miriam and Ira D. Wallach Division of Art, Prints and Photographs: Picture Collection/The New York Public Library.;
81. Library of Congress Prints and Photographs Division;
92. Reprinted with permission of the DC Public Library, Star Collection © *Washington Post*;
93. Enoch Pratt Free Library/State Library Resource Center. Hearst Communications Inc., Hearst Newspaper Division;
96. Al Monner/Oregon Historical Society Library;
102 **b.** Courtesy Boston Public Library, Leslie Jones Collection;
120. George Arents Collection/New York Public Library;
124. National Photo Company Collection/Library of Congress Prints and Photographs Division;
138 **t/c/b.** Alton H. Blackington/Special Collections and University Archives, University of Massachusetts Amherst Libraries;
145. Dick Whittington Studio/Corbis via Getty Images;
150 **tr.** George Grantham Bain Collection/Library of Congress Prints and Photographs Division;
150 **cr.** Courtesy Mary Thurston/Hartsdale Pet Cemetery;
153. USC Digital Library, Los Angeles Examiner Photographs Collection;
154. SuperStock/FIRST NATIONAL/Album/Album Archivo;
157. Everett Collection Inc.;
158. Keystone-France/Gamma-Keystone via Getty Images;
160 **t.** *Los Angeles Herald Examiner* Photo Collection/Los Angeles Public Library;
160 **b.** USC Digital Library, California Historical Society Collection;
163. Everett Collection Inc/Alamy Stock Photo;
164 **t.** CBS Photo Archive/Getty Images;
165. Eyre Powell Chamber of Commerce Photo Collection/Los Angeles Public Library;
167. Security Pacific National Bank Collection/Los Angeles Public Library;
168. Prismatic Pictures/Bridgeman Images;
176. Los Angeles Public Library;
185. The U.S. National Archives and Records Administration (165-GB-07856);
188. Harris and Ewing Photographs/Library of Congress Prints and Photographs Division;
191. Cleveland Press Collections, courtesy of the Michael Schwartz Library Special Collections, Cleveland State University;
192. The U.S. National Archives and Records Administration (111-SC-103504);
195. USC Digital Library, *Los Angeles Examiner* Photographs Collection;
201. Keystone Press/Alamy Stock Photo;
204 Courtesy of the PDSA; 205 Courtesy of the PDSA;
208. Courtesy of the PDSA;
210. Douglas Miller/Keystone/Getty Images;
215. Eastland County Museum;
216. University of Texas at Arlington Library Special Collections;
218. Overholser Historical Research Center, Fort Benton Museums;
219. Overholser Historical Research Center, Fort Benton Museums;
224. Special Collections, University of Virginia Library;
225. BNA Photographic/Alamy Stock Photo;
237. SuperStock/Album/Album Archivo;
245. Courtesy of Surrey Archives
Endpapers front: "Old Maids at a Cat's Funeral," F.G. Byron, 1789, Courtesy Library of Congress Prints and Photographs Division; back: "Old Maids at a Cat's Funeral," F.G. Byron, 1789, Courtesy Library of Congress Prints and Photographs Division

ACKNOWLEDGMENTS

The author wishes to express his gratitude to the following:

Mary Thurston, the historian at Hartsdale Pet Cemetery, and the Martin family; very special thanks to Bob Cullum and the Leslie Jones Collection, Boston Public Library; Cris Bombaugh and Julianne Mangin at Aspin Hill; Stacy Tanner and Shera Danese Falk at LA Pet Memorial Park; Florencia Van Heck at Royal Parks; Paul Frecker; Adele Mildred and David Edwards; Geoff Burn; Carys Fyson/ Huntingdon Archives; Jonnie Leger/AKG Images; Owen Phillips in Paris and the staff at the Cimetière des Chiens; Suzi Taylor/Wyoming State Archives; Kimberly Boudwin/Francisvale; Edna Clyne-Rekhy; Rebecca Buckingham and the PDSA; Robin Hutton; Lisa Graham/ Animal Rescue League of Boston; Wendy Horowitz/Los Angeles Public Library; Jeffrey Vallance; the staff of Sea Breeze Pet Cemetery; Katie Grim/Museum of Riverside; Carolyn McHenry; Dorothy Yanchak; Heather Kamitakahara/City of Surrey; Robert Thomson/Presidio Trust.

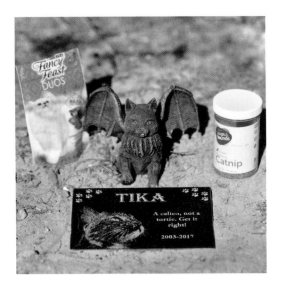

Front cover
A broken cross now marks the grave of Beauty at
Friendship Grove, Hornell, New York. Photo by the author.

Back cover
Starlet Doris Hill at the Los Angeles Pet Memorial Park.
Courtesy Everett Collection Inc.

Page 2 Monument honoring the dogs owned by the
founders of Clara Glen Pet Cemetery in New Jersey.

Pages 4–5 Sign surrounded by graves at the entrance
to the off-the-grid pet cemetery near Bishop, California.

Page 6 As night falls, battery-powered lights illuminate
a grave for several cats in Helsinki, Finland.

Pages 16–17 Last respects in (clockwise from upper left):
Denpasar, Bali; Catalina Island, California; Cairo; Helsinki;
Taipei; Los Angeles; Juárez, Mexico; La Paz, Bolivia;
Bangkok; Salida, Colorado.

Page 18 A woman strolls the Hyde Park cemetery with two
Great Danes; from the 1926 book *Wonderful London*.

Page 60 Bunny was depicted carrying a newspaper under
his paws at Aspin Hill Pet Cemetery in Maryland.

Page 98 Dog's grave at Cottesbrooke Gardens,
Northampton; the inscription is copied from an original
recorded in Scotland.

Page 142 Tippy, at Hinsdale Pet Cemetery near Chicago,
was "Hound Dog" enough to have befriended Elvis Presley.

Page 180 One of many tributes offered at the War Dog
Memorial in South Lyon, Michigan.

Page 212 Rip—or whoever this horned frog might actually
be—currently on display in Eastland, Texas.

Page 256 One of the author's own, Tika, a cat laid to rest
in Winterhaven, California.

First published in the United Kingdom in 2024 by
Thames & Hudson Ltd, 181A High Holborn, London WC1V 7QX

First published in the United States of America in 2024 by
Thames & Hudson Inc., 500 Fifth Avenue, New York, New York 10110

Faithful Unto Death © 2024 Thames & Hudson Ltd, London

Text © 2024 Paul Koudounaris

For image copyright information see p. 253

Design by Barnbrook

British Library Cataloguing-in-Publication Data
A catalogue record for this book is available from the British
Library

Library of Congress Control Number 2024935634

ISBN 978-0-500-02751-6

Printed in China by R R Donnelley

MIX
Paper | Supporting
responsible forestry
FSC® C144853

Be the first to know about our new releases,
exclusive content and author events by visiting
thamesandhudson.com
thamesandhudsonusa.com
thamesandhudson.com.au